50 HEALTHY AND DELICIOUS RECIPES FOR

DIABETIC COOKING

50 HEALTHY AND DELICIOUS RECIPES FOR
DIABETIC
COOKING

Each recipe shown step by step in more than 240 photographs

Michelle Berriedale-Johnson

southwater

This edition is published by Southwater, an imprint of Anness Publishing Ltd, Hermes House,
88–89 Blackfriars Road, London SE1 8HA; tel. 020 7401 2077; fax 020 7633 9499
www.southwaterbooks.com; www.annesspublishing.com

If you like the images in this book and would like to investigate using them for publishing, promotions
or advertising, please visit our website www.practicalpictures.com for more information.

UK agent: The Manning Partnership Ltd; tel. 01225 478444;
fax 01225 478440; sales@manning-partnership.co.uk
UK distributor: Grantham Book Services Ltd; tel. 01476 541080;
fax 01476 541061; orders@gbs.tbs-ltd.co.uk
North American agent/distributor: National Book Network;
tel. 301 459 3366; fax 301 429 5746; www.nbnbooks.com
Australian agent/distributor: Pan Macmillan Australia;
tel. 1300 135 113; fax 1300 135 103; customer.service@macmillan.com.au
New Zealand agent/distributor: David Bateman Ltd;
tel. (09) 415 7664; fax (09) 415 8892

Publisher: Joanna Lorenz
Senior Cookery Editor: Linda Fraser
Indexer: Pat Coward
Nutritional Analysis: Helen Daniels
Designer: Ian Sandom
Photography: James Duncan
Food for Photography: Nicola Fowler
Styling: Rosie Hopper
Production Controller: Joanna King

ETHICAL TRADING POLICY

Because of our ongoing ecological investment programme, you, as our customer, can have the pleasure and reassurance of
knowing that a tree is being cultivated on your behalf to naturally replace the materials used to make the book you are holding.
For further information about this scheme, go to www.annesspublishing.com/trees

Previously published as *Kitchen Doctor: Diabetic Cooking for Health*

PUBLISHER'S NOTE

Although the advice and information in this book are believed to be accurate and true at the time of going to press, neither the
authors nor the publisher can accept any legal responsibility or liability for any errors or omissions that may be made.

NOTES

For all recipes, quantities are given in
both metric and imperial measures
and, where appropriate, in standard
cups and spoons. Follow one set of
measures, but not a mixture, because
they are not interchangeable.
Standard spoon and cup measures are
level. 1 tsp = 5ml, 1 tbsp = 15ml,
1 cup = 250ml/8fl oz.

Australian standard tablespoons are
20ml. Australian readers should use
3 tsp in place of 1 tbsp for measuring
small quantities.

American pints are 16fl oz/2 cups.
American readers should use
20fl oz/2.5 cups in place of 1 pint
when measuring liquids.

Electric oven temperatures in this book
are for conventional ovens. When using a
fan oven, the temperature will probably
need to be reduced by about 10–20°C/
20–40°F. Since ovens vary, you should
check with your manufacturer's instruction book for guidance.

Medium (US large) eggs are used
unless otherwise stated.

Main front cover image shows Avocado and Strawberry Salad – for recipe, see page 28.

CONTENTS

INTRODUCTION

By the time you pick up this book you (or a friend, child or parent) may already have been diagnosed as diabetic, so you may have a pretty good idea of what being diabetic is and what it involves. However, since understanding a situation is often the key to coping with it, it may be worth reviewing what you actually know.

Don't be intimidated by the wealth of rather technical information in the next few pages. The principles of dealing with diabetes are really very simple and, once you have got the hang of them, quite easy to cope with.

Most diabetics, especially those recently diagnosed, live very healthy and normal lives – some go on to excel in sports, which many non-diabetics could not dream of. So, take heart – and read on.

WHAT IS DIABETES?

The name, *diabetes mellitus*, comes from two Greek words (*diabetes* – a siphon; *mellitus* – honey, because the urine of a diabetic tastes sweet) and describes a condition in which the sugar (or glucose) circulating in the blood cannot be absorbed properly. This results in abnormally high blood glucose levels, which can cause both short- and long-term problems.

To explain in a bit more detail: Glucose (a form of sugar) is the body's main fuel – it provides us with our energy. We absorb glucose from starchy and sugary carbohydrate foods, such as potatoes, rice and beans, breads, biscuits, cakes, sugar and sweets. As we chew, enzymes in saliva start breaking down these foods, a process that is continued by the acids in the stomach. As the food progresses on into the gut, digestive juices from the pancreas and gall bladder get to work, and by the time the food reaches the bowel it has been broken down into simple particles (including glucose), which are absorbed through the bowel wall into the bloodstream. The glucose in the bloodstream moves on through the liver where much of it is stored for future use, and into body cells where it is either burned up to provide energy or stored for future use.

However, the glucose in the blood cannot enter the cells in the liver or any other part of the body unless a chemical (insulin) effectively "opens the door" into those cells. Insulin is a hormone that is manufactured in the pancreas (the glandular organ that lies behind the stomach but in front of the backbone) and stored there until rising glucose levels in the bloodstream set off a chemical reaction, which releases the insulin. Once in the bloodstream, the insulin links into the body's cells through what are called insulin receptors (a procedure which is rather like two space ships docking). This linkage precipitates chemical changes in the cell walls, which allow the glucose through into the cell where it can be converted into energy.

In a non-diabetic this monitoring and replenishment process happens automatically so that the body's cells are continually fed with sufficient glucose for their energy needs, while excess glucose is stored in the cells. In a diabetic the system fails either because the pancreas does not produce any insulin at all (Insulin Dependent Diabetes Mellitus or IDDM) or because the pancreas' supply of insulin is reduced, the supply of insulin receptors is reduced or neither functions very efficiently (Non Insulin Dependent Diabetes or NIDDM).

Despite years of research no one has discovered why it is that the pancreas should (as in the onset of IDDM) suddenly cease to produce insulin, although it would appear that some people can have a genetic predisposition to diabetes. For susceptible individuals, a viral disease can act on the immune system to make it turn upon the "beta" cells in the pancreas, which manufacture the insulin, and destroy them. In NIDDM there seems to be not only a genetic but a radical

Above: Children and young adults are more likely to be insulin dependent diabetics than non insulin dependent diabetics.

predisposition: NIDDM is four times more common in Asian communities than in the rest of the population of Britain, for example. However, with NIDDM, which occurs mainly in older and frequently overweight people (IDDM usually occurs in thin children and people under 30), there does appear to be a link with obesity. Other possible contributory causes to NIDDM in later years could be pancreatic damage through surgery or alcohol abuse; glucose intolerance during pregnancy, which may disappear after the baby is born but leaves a predisposition to diabetes during later pregnancies or in later life; long-term use of some steroids, which raise the amount of glucose in the blood; and overactivity of the thyroid.

DIAGNOSIS AND SYMPTOMS

Diagnosis of insulin dependent diabetes is normally fairly straightforward as the symptoms, although varied, are pretty obvious and can even be quite dramatic. Non insulin dependent diabetes is another matter, since the fall in insulin production may occur over a number of years and the symptoms may be quite slight. Some people with NIDDM have no symptoms at all.

DIAGNOSIS

If you go to a doctor complaining of any of these symptoms (right), he or she will normally check for diabetes.

The first test might be for excess glucose in the urine although, since the glucose levels in the urine tend to fluctuate (and some people have a low threshold so register as having above the normal level without actually being diabetic), the existence of such an excess is not absolute proof of diabetes. It is more usual to be sent for a blood glucose test. This blood will be taken from a vein, not a finger prick. By the time blood reaches the finger through the small blood vessels or capillaries, it has used up some of the glucose it was originally carrying so does not give an accurate picture. So it is important to measure the glucose in blood taken from a vein (the venous plasma glucose concentration). The normal glucose concentration that you would expect to find, according to World Health Organization (WHO) criteria, is below 7.8 millimols per litre.

A diabetic, according to the WHO criteria, is one whose "venous plasma glucose concentration" when they have been fasting, remains at 7.8mmol/litre, but rises to above 11.1mmol/litre on a random blood sample. Between "normal" and "diabetic" they list a third category of those with "impaired glucose tolerance" (7.8mmol/litre fasting and between 7.8 and 11.1mmol/litre on a random test). These people may return to normal, may go on to develop

full-blown diabetes or remain at the same level. They should, however, follow a diabetic regime and keep themselves as healthy as possible.

TREATMENT

Although serious, even IDDM has become a treatable condition following the arrival of injectable insulin. Provided you are prepared to stick to your regime, there is no reason why you should not lead a full life.

The key to the management and treatment of both IDDM and NIDDM is to take over the job normally performed by the insulin in the body and keep your blood sugar levels normal. Allowing them to get too high, or too low, can cause a variety of problems and is to be avoided. This does not mean getting paranoid about blood sugar levels or diet – merely keeping a sensible watch on both.

For NIDDMs a change in diet, possibly in conjunction with medication to lower blood glucose levels, will frequently achieve the desired result. Indeed, changes to the diet may improve the health of an individual to such an extent that the onset of their diabetes may be viewed as something of a blessing.

IDDMs have benefited from the development of sophisticated blood testing techniques. These usually involve taking a drop of blood from the finger or ear lobe and have made it much easier to control blood glucose levels, either by changing the diet or the insulin dose.

Whether you have been diagnosed as being an insulin dependent diabetic or a diabetic who is non insulin dependent, your doctor will instruct you in the use of your drugs, insulin and glucose testing equipment. He or she will also give you dietary guidance or send you to a dietitian. The principles and practices for a good diabetic diet are described later in this introduction and further amplified in the recipe section.

SYMPTOMS

Thirst (polydipsia) and passing large quantities of urine (polyuria)
If the levels of glucose in the blood are too high, the kidneys no longer filter all the glucose and some escapes into the urine. The extra glucose thickens the urine, it draws extra water with it to help it to flow through the kidneys, and this causes the bladder to fill. The individual needs to urinate often and in copious amounts. At the same time the body becomes dehydrated, which leads to a terrible thirst.

Constipation
As the body becomes more dehydrated, constipation becomes almost inevitable.

Tiredness and weight loss
Since our bodies acquire their energy from glucose, anyone whose body cannot access the glucose circulating in the blood will be short of energy and therefore tired. In an effort to replace this energy, the body will break down other cells/body tissues thus causing a weight loss that can be dramatic.

Blurred vision
Excess sugar in the blood makes it thick and syrupy. In some diabetics, this can upset the focusing of the eyes – their vision becomes blurred.

Infections
When the blood becomes thick and syrupy due to the presence of excess glucose, this may also effect the functioning of the immune system. The undiagnosed diabetic may be prone to all kinds of infections, including skin eruptions, urinary tract infections, such as thrush or cystitis, and chest infections.

Pins and needles
Changes in the blood glucose levels may also affect nerve functions, resulting in tingling or pins and needles in the hands or feet.

ALTERNATIVE THERAPIES

Once the pancreas has given up on insulin production, it can very rarely be "kicked back into action". However, certain alternative or complementary therapies can stimulate pancreatic function, improve the body's insulin response and moderate glucose levels, so they are worth considering both in cases of non insulin dependent diabetes and in the immediate aftermath of the onset of insulin dependent diabetes, when there may still be some residual function in the pancreas.

Equally important is the diabetic's need to keep as fit and healthy – in both mind and body – as possible. It is recognized that stress does more damage to our health than almost anything else – and that many alternative therapies are very helpful in dealing with stress. Yoga, meditation, reflexology, aromatherapy and massage are the best-known stress relievers, but many people find spiritual healers, colour therapists or practising T'ai Chi just as helpful.

CHINESE MEDICINE

The Chinese have recognized diabetes as a disease for many thousands of years. However, Chinese medicine approaches the body, bodily functions and bodily malfunctions from an entirely different angle from Western medicine. To a Chinese doctor, diabetes is a sign of disharmony in the body, whose symptoms appear in the upper body (raging thirst, dry mouth, drinking huge quantities), middle body (large appetite and excessive eating accompanied by weight loss and constipation) and lower body (copious urination, progressive weight loss, etc).

Chinese medical treatment would therefore concentrate on restoring the harmony within the individual with the aim of improving the symptoms and addressing the disease.

Even if this approach does not directly affect insulin production or control, improving the body's natural harmony should improve the diabetic's general health and therefore their ability to cope well with diabetes. However, insulin dependent diabetics must not change their insulin regime if they attend a Chinese physician, except on the express instruction of their diabetes specialist.

RELAXATION AND MASSAGE THERAPIES

It is recognized that stress plays a significant role in the development of diabetes. Any therapy that reduces stress and helps you to relax is therefore likely to have a beneficial effect upon control of your diabetes and your general health.

Yoga and meditation have been found to have a positive impact on blood glucose levels, while moderate exercise helps insulin to work more efficiently in the body.

Reflexology helps to tone and relax the body and, although it cannot address the cause of diabetes, it can alleviate some of the side effects.

Left: Yoga and meditation are both said to reduce blood glucose levels by helping you to relax and reduce stress.

SELF MASSAGE

Aromatherapy (massage with essential herbal oils) is not only relaxing, but can also improve circulation and therefore help to heal the leg and foot ulcers to which some diabetics are prone.

The therapeutic potential of aromatherapy oils, although recognized in the past, has been largely ignored until recently. However, it is now realized that concentrated oils (made from plants and herbs that filled our ancestors' medicine chests) can be very helpful for many specific complaints.

Essential oils are easily absorbed through the skin into the bloodstream and so are particularly effective for circulatory problems. Some oils, such as hyssop, are good for the circulation as a whole; others, such as grapefruit, lemon, lime, fennel and white birch, are lymphatic stimulants; while spike lavender, rosemary, eucalyptus, peppermint and thyme stimulate sluggish circulation. Massage is a good way to apply essential oils as it is relaxing, and it also ensures that the oils are effectively absorbed.

LEG AND FOOT MASSAGE

Self-massage is relatively easy and can help considerably in reducing stiffness and sluggishness of blood flow in the legs.

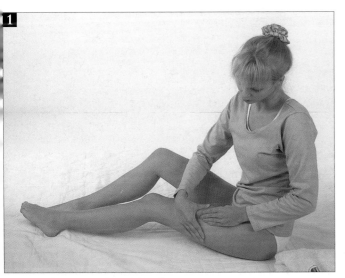

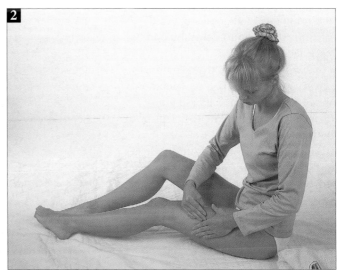

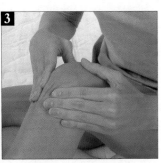

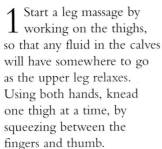

1 Start a leg massage by working on the thighs, so that any fluid in the calves will have somewhere to go as the upper leg relaxes. Using both hands, knead one thigh at a time, by squeezing between the fingers and thumb.

2 Squeeze with each hand alternately for the best effect, working from the knee to the hip and back. Repeat on the other thigh.

3 Around the knees, do a similar kneading action but just using the fingers for a lighter effect and working in smaller circles.

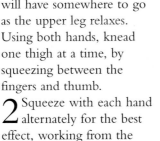

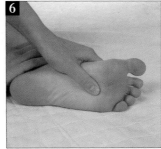

4 Bend your leg, and if possible raise the foot on to a chair or handy ledge. With your thumbs, work on the back of each calf with a circular, kneading action. Repeat this action a few times on each leg, each time working from the ankle up to the knee.

5 Squeeze the foot with your hands, loosening up the muscles and gently stretching the arch.

6 To complete the massage, use firm pressure with your thumb to stretch the foot. Repeat on the other foot.

FOOD AND HERBAL MEDICINES

Certain foods and herbs, although they cannot reinstate pancreatic function, can help the pancreas to function more efficiently. They may also improve the absorption of insulin and lead to better control of glucose levels in the blood by the body and to improved circulation. This may, in part, be due to the nutrients found in these foods and herbs (see Nutritional Medicine below), but there is increasing evidence that certain foods and herbs have special health-giving properties, which cannot be entirely attributed to their vitamin or mineral content.

FOODS WITH HEALTH-GIVING PROPERTIES

• Whole oats, onions, globe artichokes and pulses all have the ability to reduce blood sugar.
• Wheat germ, underripe bananas, turkey, fish, walnuts, red peppers and cruciferous vegetables, such as broccoli and cauliflower (all good sources of Vitamin B6), help to control blood sugar levels.
• Shellfish, lean meat, wholegrain cereals, pulses, pumpkin seeds and nuts are all high in chromium and zinc (diabetics are commonly deficient in both minerals).
• Blueberries have been found to help in the control of diabetic retinopathy.
• Wheatgerm, sunflower seeds, rapeseed oils, almonds and sweet potatoes (all containing high levels of Vitamin E) have been shown to help improve diabetic circulation and neuropathy.
• Fresh nettle juice has been used since Roman times to stimulate the circulation, while dandelions have an equally lengthy pedigree for the stimulation of the liver (where glucose is stored).

Above: Dandelions have been used for years as a stimulant for the liver.

NUTRITIONAL MEDICINE

Effects of nutrient deficiencies
Although it has long been recognized that we need a wide range of vitamins and minerals for our bodies to function efficiently, there is a growing belief that many of today's degenerative illnesses, such as diabetes, could be caused by serious deficiencies in micronutrients, such as vitamins, minerals and amino acids. These deficiencies, it is argued, have resulted from our eating over-processed foods, living in a highly polluted environment and subjecting ourselves to hitherto unknown levels of stress. Research is going on all the time and continues to reveal links between certain degenerative conditions and particular nutrient deficiencies.
Chromium is an essential trace element. Although it is only present in minute quantities in the body, it appears to be necessary for blood sugar control and the proper action of insulin. Unfortunately chromium is removed from refined carbohydrates during processing. Chromium is difficult to take as a supplement but is absorbed from brewer's yeast, black pepper, calf's liver, wheat germ, wholemeal bread and cheese.
Vitamins B6 and B12 can both help blood sugar control. Vitamin B12 levels can be reduced by certain diabetic drugs, so it is useful to include sources of this vitamin (lean meat and dairy produce) in the diet.

Above: Nutritional supplements can help to ensure that you are getting the right amounts of some vitamins, minerals and essential fatty acids.

Vitamin C is known to strengthen fragile blood capillaries, especially in the eye, and to reduce elevated cholesterol levels – both conditions that affect diabetics.
Zinc, magnesium and potassium are all very important for diabetics, but levels can be seriously depleted through excess urination. Zinc is important for combating infections such as eczema, acne and thrush, many of which afflict diabetics. Magnesium is also important for the proper functioning of the kidneys.
Essential fatty acids There is increasing evidence that a diabetic's absorption of essential fatty acids may be impeded by raised blood sugar or insulin deficiency so taking a supplement, such as Evening Primrose oil, may help prevent diabetic complications.

KEEPING BLOOD GLUCOSE LEVELS NORMAL

The ideal state for a diabetic is for blood sugar levels to remain normal. Careful monitoring of these, a good diet and medication where necessary are basic strategies. However, many other aspects of the diabetic's life may impinge on his or her blood sugar levels.

BLOOD GLUCOSE LEVELS

Changing exercise levels, for example, can affect both the efficiency of insulin uptake and the rate at which the sugar in the blood is used up. Stress of any kind may cause adrenalin release that will increase the level of sugar in the blood. Infections, injuries or operations are seen by the body as stress. The body reacts by releasing adrenalin or other hormones into the bloodstream, and these again push up the sugar levels. Pregnancy causes changes in blood sugar levels, as do monthly periods and the menopause. Medical drugs, especially steroids and some diuretics and anti-depressants, can also affect blood sugar levels. If any of these factors apply, it is essential to monitor your blood sugar levels even more carefully than usual, adapting your diet or adjusting your insulin dose or the levels of the drug you take to lower blood glucose, in consultation with your doctor, if necessary.

Serious fluctuations in glucose levels cause hypoglycaemia (too little sugar) and hyperglycaemia (too much sugar) and have very specific symptoms, which need to be treated immediately. If dramatic rises (and, more especially, falls) in blood sugar are treated immediately, there are unlikely to be long-term effects. However, persistent slightly raised blood sugar levels of about 8–19mmol/litre do have a number of serious consequences in terms of health.

CORONARY HEART DISEASE

Elevated triglycerides (fats in the blood) are a common feature of poorly controlled diabetes and add greatly to the risk of coronary heart disease (when the arteries supplying blood to the heart "fur up", thus depriving the heart muscle of the blood it needs to function properly), so diabetics need to be particularly careful about eating a low-fat diet and ensuring that they are not overweight.

STROKE

High blood pressure is another area which diabetics need to watch. Keeping their weight normal, stopping smoking and eating a low-fat, low-salt diet will usually help a great deal to minimize the risk of strokes.

Below: Pregnancy will affect blood glucose levels, which need to be monitored.

NEUROPATHY

Diabetic neuropathy is very common in long-term and poorly controlled diabetics. Although there are many variations, neuropathy happens when the nerve ends become damaged (as a result of excess glucose flowing through the capillaries or small veins). Neuropathy normally affects the hands and feet (tingling or pins and needles in the hands and feet is one of the symptoms of diabetes) and can, over a period, result in loss of all feeling in the extremities.

Left: Exercise, such as jogging, increases the rate at which sugar in the blood is used up – to prevent a dangerous dip in your blood glucose level, eat a small carbohydrate snack before, or straight after, any exercise.

Neuropathy presents two problems. One is that the circulation to the more remote areas of the body gets worse and this can lead to infected wounds, bad healing and, in the worst cases, gangrene. Feet and legs are especially prone to damage and need to be looked after and monitored with great care. The other problem is that the feet lose all sensation. This not only affects balance and the ability to walk properly but also means that the sufferer is at risk of injury, perhaps by being scalded by getting into too hot a bath, because their feet have become so insensitive to temperature.

Diabetics can also suffer some damage to their "autonomic nerves". These are the nerves that carry the instructions to the various organs, such as heart, kidneys, bladder and bowels, and tell them what to do. Damage to these autonomic nerves can result in poor bowel or bladder control, failure of the stomach to empty properly and similar problems. Normally all these functions will return to normal when the blood glucose levels are also returned to normal.

KIDNEY AND EYE DAMAGE

The kidneys and the eyes are two areas of the body filled with capillaries or tiny blood vessels that are especially prone to diabetic damage. Excess blood sugar can "clog" up both areas, but whereas kidney damage may be reversed or at least controlled by diet and good blood glucose control, damage to the eyes may be irreversible. Maintaining good control of blood glucose levels will minimize the damage. It is particularly important that diabetics have very regular eye checks and that these should include examination of the retina.

SKIN PROBLEMS

Because raised blood sugar makes one more prone to infection, especially skin infection, badly controlled diabetes will often result in boils, pimples, spots and rashes. Most of these will respond well to good diet and improved control.

This disturbing list of symptoms may sound like a life sentence, but diabetics should remember that most of them only occur when they do not look after themselves. These days, a diabetic diet is almost identical to the healthy diet recommended for all of us – so the diabetic should not be singled out as an oddity. Because of the huge improvement in both monitoring and injection techniques, even insulin dependent diabetics can check their blood sugar levels and administer their insulin both quickly and discreetly. However, this does not mean that you should keep your diabetes a secret. For a start, there is no reason to as you can live a perfectly full life with diabetes. Secondly, friends, colleagues and even strangers need to know that you are diabetic in case you should suffer a hyper- or hypoglycaemic attack. This is easily dealt with, but very frightening if you or others do not know what is going on. Consider wearing a diabetic bracelet or tag.

All diabetes does require is that you take it seriously and are organized about dealing with it. You must be rigorous about checking your glucose levels, you must always make sure that you have your insulin or drugs available and you must always ensure that you have extra glucose or carbohydrate food should you need it. Finally, you must be aware that your body is more sensitive to change than that of someone without diabetes so you must pay attention to what it tells you in terms of "feeling different" or unwell. Your body is the best possible monitor of its own condition, so it is important to listen to it!

HYPER- AND HYPOGLYCAEMIA

Hyper- and hypoglycaemia occur when blood sugar levels rise too high (hyper) or fall too low (hypo).

HYPERGLYCAEMIA

The symptoms of hyperglycaemia are usually less dramatic than those of hypoglycaemia, but because tissue damage may result if the blood sugar levels remain too high (usually over 11–12mmol/litre), it is important to get the levels down quickly.

Elevated levels of blood sugar can be the result of uncontrolled long-term diabetes, but there can also be more immediate causes. Forgetting to take your insulin or blood glucose drugs will cause your blood sugar levels to rise, as will eating much more than you usually do – or eating a fattier or more sugary meal than normal.

Reducing the amount of exercise you usually take could affect glucose levels. An infection, illness, operation or accident could all cause blood sugar levels to rise, as can pregnancy and menstruation. Careful monitoring will reveal the raised levels quickly – anything over 11mmol/litre is undesirable – and changes in insulin, drugs or diet should get you back to normal.

HYPOGLYCAEMIA

Hypoglycaemia can occur in non-diabetics whose blood sugar levels fall too low; the official definition is below 2.5mmol/litre. However, this reaction is most frequently seen in diabetics who have taken more insulin than they need or eaten too little – or exercised too much – relative to their last dose of insulin or glucose-lowering drugs.

Although the symptoms of hypoglycaemia can be dramatic, its results are seldom serious, and it is extremely easy to treat. All you need is a rapid intake of sugar in the form of glucose tablets (Dextrose, Dextro), sugar lumps, honey, candy, fruit juice or sweet biscuits. Even when the symptoms are quite extreme, the diabetic will be back to normal in a matter of minutes.

Above: Glucose tablets are a simple and speedy remedy to mild hypoglycaemia.

However, they then need to back up the instant injection of glucose with more solid food, as the excess insulin will quickly absorb the initial blast of glucose and will need something further to work on.

The problem with hypoglycaemia is that the brain is utterly dependent on an adequate supply of glucose to function properly. The first sign that a diabetic is suffering from a "hypo" may be a failure in his or her logical reasoning powers. This can manifest itself as a refusal to accept that they may be suffering from a hypo – which is why it is particularly important for friends and colleagues to know that they are diabetic (and for the diabetic to carry a card or consider wearing an identifying bracelet or badge), so that if their hypo symptoms take the form of denial, someone else can get a glucose tablet into their mouth.

Hypo symptoms vary enormously, but they often include lack of concentration, difficulty in making even simple decisions or a feeling of being muddled. A common feeling is that you must finish whatever you are doing, even though you are feeling odd. This is particularly dangerous if you are driving a car, so diabetics must make every effort to recognize and combat this compulsion.

Hypos can often cause behavioural changes and quite violent mood swings. Coordination may also be impaired. They may stagger as if drunk and have difficulty in performing the simplest task – like unwrapping a glucose tablet!

If unrecognized and untreated, a hypo will eventually cause a diabetic to lose consciousness, but even then an injection of glucagon (the antidote to insulin) will bring the diabetic round to the point where they can be fed a proper dose of glucose.

Since symptoms are so varied, it is important that diabetics are aware of changes in their physical or mental states, that they monitor their blood sugar levels regularly, compensate for any changes in their daily routine and always carry glucose tablets (or the equivalent) with them. Long-term diabetics should be aware that over time symptoms of hypo decrease so that their blood sugar may fall without them having any symptoms at all.

A FEW WORDS OF WARNING

• Ignore rising blood sugar levels at your peril. Your body's reaction will not be as rapid as with low levels, but if ignored rising blood sugar levels can put you into a coma.

• Never give up your insulin or drug regime – even if you are vomiting. The greater the stress on the body, the greater its need for insulin to combat rising blood sugar levels. Vomiting is serious for a diabetic, so maintain your drug regime and consult a doctor.

• Because the body is infinitely adaptable, some people will feel quite ill when their blood sugar is only slightly raised, while others will still feel relatively okay with seriously high levels. Moreover, long-term undiagnosed diabetics may have got used to having high levels of sugar in their blood so they will not even notice feeling ill.

• It is particularly important to monitor your blood sugar levels on a regular basis, even if you feel fine.

HEALTHY EATING

Diet is the backbone of both insulin dependent and non insulin dependent diabetic management, and the first line of attack in stabilizing blood sugar control. Today, the diabetic diet varies little from the diet that everyone should be eating: to eat at least five portions of fruit and vegetables each day, to take in less than 30 per cent of calories from fat (with most of it coming from mono- and polyunsaturated fats), to reduce the intake of salt (sodium) and sweet foods and to eat plenty of fibre.

THE "OLD" APPROACH

Because sugar is derived from carbohydrates, when the mechanism of carbohydrate absorption was less well understood than it is today, it was thought that diabetics should avoid all carbohydrates. This meant that they had to live on a high-protein, high-fat diet and suffer the side-effects, such as high blood pressure, now associated with such a diet. Moreover, a high-fat diet caused them to gain weight.

Below: Protein is needed for growth and cell repair – wholegrain rice, beans, lentils, tofu and walnuts are all good sources.

TODAY'S APPROACH

Research over the last 25 years has turned this thinking on its head, and, although present-day diabetics still have to monitor their diet and their carbohydrate intake fairly carefully, they are now encouraged to eat plenty of the right kind of carbohydrate foods, while even a small amount of sugar as such is no longer entirely out of the question.

The food that we eat is made up of proteins, fats, carbohydrates, fibre, micronutrients (vitamins and minerals) and water. The last four (fibre, vitamins, minerals and water) are all essential for the proper functioning of the body but they do not provide us with energy as such (measured in kilo-calories or kilo-joules). This we need to get from proteins, fats and carbohydrates.

PROTEINS

Proteins (found in pulses, peas and beans, soya products, such as tofu, nuts, cereals, meat, fish and dairy products, such as cheese, milk and cream) are essential for growth in children and for cell repair in adults. We need to get up to 20 per cent of our daily energy intake in the form of proteins.

FATS

Fats (found primarily in meat and dairy products, but also in vegetable and fish oils and nuts) are essential to the proper functioning of the body. However, we need the right kind of fat and the right amount. The average Western diet contains far too much of the "wrong" kind of fat – saturated – which leads to obesity, heart problems and strokes. The recommended maximum number of daily calories which should come from fat is between 30 and 35 per cent. Unfortunately many Westerners obtain well over 40 per cent of their calories from fat.

Fats are broken down into saturated fats (mainly from the fat on meat, but also dairy products, such as cream, full-fat milk, butter and cheese, and nuts), polyunsaturated fats and mono-unsaturated fats (from vegetable oils such as olive oil and sunflower oil and from fish oils).

The subject of fats is a very complex one, but for the purposes of the diabetic diet the main thing to

Above: Sunflower oil (left) contains mostly polyunsaturated fats, while olive oil is made up of mainly monounsaturated fats.

remember is that saturated fats are to be avoided. These are more likely to cause excess cholesterol to be deposited in the arteries and, because they are higher in calories, obesity is a likely outcome. Diabetics may have high fat concentrations in their blood anyhow (making them more vulnerable to arteriosclerosis), so they should avoid making these levels even higher.

Above: Many different foods, such as (clockwise from top right) milk, pistachio nuts, butter, almonds, cream and cheese, contain fats. Dairy products, such as cheese, butter and milk are sources of saturated fats, which should be avoided by diabetics, while foods such as nuts are good sources of polyunsaturated fats, which, like monoun-saturated fats are much more beneficial.

CARBOHYDRATES

Carbohydrates (known in "diet-speak" as CHOs) also come in different guises – simple and complex carbohydrates. **Simple (refined or sugary) carbo-hydrates** consist of various forms of what we know broadly as sugar or sucrose. In fact, sucrose is made up from glucose and fructose (fruit sugar). Both are essential for providing us with energy, but glucose is particularly important as the brain depends upon it to function efficiently.

Complex carbohydrates (unrefined carbohydrates) are to be found in starchy foods such as pulses (beans), oats, rice, potatoes and bread. Complex carbohydrates are made up of simple carbohydrates, glucose (see above) and fibres. These fibres may be soluble or insoluble. Soluble fibre is found in pulses, beans and legumes; it breaks down into a sort of gluey solution, which contains the carbo-hydrate. Insoluble fibre, such as that found in bran and such vegetables as celery and cabbage, has no nutritional value but is used by the body to move food through the system and to push out what is not wanted as waste.

Once they enter the digestive system, complex carbohydrates are broken down by the digestive juices into their components parts – sucrose and fibre. For a diabetic, the virtue of a carbohydrate made up of sucrose and soluble fibre (pulses, peas and beans) is that the gluey solution into which the soluble fibre turns prevents the system from absorbing the glucose too fast, thus giving the diabetic's impaired glucose handling system more time to absorb it. The disadvantage of simple carbohydrates (sugar or sucrose) is that they are absorbed almost immediately into the bloodstream, causing sudden glucose "peaks".

Although studies suggest that if it is eaten along with lots of starchy, high-fibre carbohydrate, a small amount of pure sugar can be successfully absorbed by some diabetics without creating glucose peaks, medical advice would still be to avoid sugar whenever possible. "Sugar" in this context would include sugar itself (in tea or coffee etc), sweets and candies, jams and jellies, cake and biscuits sweetened with sugar or fructose, and sweetened fizzy drinks.

"DIABETIC" FOODS

Medical advice is also to avoid expensive proprietary diabetic foods. Although their actual sucrose content may be lower than that of the foods they are meant to replace, they may use fructose or sorbitol as sweeteners (there is little medical evidence that fructose is any better for diabetics than glucose, and sorbitol can cause bowel problems if eaten in large quantities). Finally, these foods may make up for their low-sugar content by having a high-fat content!

Below: Unrefined or complex carbohydrates, which are found in such foods as (clockwise from top right) wholemeal bread, potatoes, oats, haricot beans, rice and lentils, are absorbed more slowly into the bloodstream.

THE DIABETIC'S DAY-TO-DAY DIET

The first thing that the diabetic must remember is that, because the body's ability to absorb sugar is impaired, the system must never be "overloaded". In practice, this means that he or she should have three regularly spaced, moderately sized meals, usually breakfast, lunch and dinner, with two or three regular snacks in between, such as elevenses, mid-afternoon tea and a snack at bed time. For an insulin dependent diabetic the meals must be timed to come 15–30 minutes after the insulin injection so that the insulin has had time to be absorbed into the bloodstream and is ready to cope with the food.

If you are a newly diagnosed diabetic and have led a rather disorganized life you may find forcing yourself to stick to specific times for meals difficult, but it will prove worth it. And you can console yourself with the thought that if the rest of us ate on a more regular basis we would all feel a lot better too!

BALANCE
A diabetic should try to ensure that each meal or snack is balanced to include proteins, fats and carbohydrates. This is not difficult to achieve, as many snacks naturally contain all three components in varying amounts. A ham sandwich, for example, includes protein (ham), fat (butter, spread) and carbohydrate (bread).

It is important that the diabetic does not miss out on any one element, especially the carbohydrate. Diabetics used to be given a list of what were known as "carbohydrate exchanges", which allocated a carbohydrate value to each food. They then had to work out how much carbohydrate was in each meal they ate, allocate their meal allowance of carbohydrate and devise a "swap" system if they wanted to change any element of this diet. Today, although diabetic practitioners still allot a total carbohydrate allowance to be spread over the day (based on the diabetic's own lifestyle, eating patterns, medication, etc), this does not need to be as rigid as the old exchange system.

AVOIDING EXCESSIVE CALORIE INTAKE
Whereas insulin dependent diabetics are often very thin, non insulin diabetics, especially long-term ones, tend to obesity – partly of course because the traditional diabetic diet was high in fat and protein. However, it is really important for diabetics to keep their weight down so as to minimize circulatory and other diseases.

As anyone knows who has tried to diet, the only long-term answer is to reduce the total amount of food that you eat and change the nature of that food.

Reducing the amount of sugar in your diet will set you well on the way; reducing the amount of fat, especially saturated fat, in your diet will help even more. And reduction does not necessarily mean total deprivation!

Right: Fizzy, sweetened drinks, full-sugar jam, sweet biscuits, confectionery, chocolate and cakes aren't completely banned, but consumption of these high-calorie foods should be kept to a minimum.

REDUCING SUGAR

Most diabetic practitioners would prefer their patients to stop sweetening their tea and coffee. However, if the thought is too terrible to contemplate, intense sweeteners, such as Aspartame (NutraSweet, Canderel) or Saccharin (Sweet'n'Low, Hermesetas) are better than sugar, but their consumption should be kept to a minimum.

Sugar in drinks other than coffee and tea – fizzy drinks, colas, etc – should be avoided. Not only do these fizzy drinks give an instant glucose hit (bad for diabetic control), but they are also very calorific (the average cola contains the equivalent of seven teaspoons of sugar). Fizzy water or fresh fruit juice diluted with water are preferred – or, if desperate, the diabetic should stick with low-calorie artificially sweetened, fizzy drinks.

Sugar in baking can almost always be replaced with dried or fresh fruits, as is amply illustrated in the recipes that follow. Although fruit contains fructose, this is buried in fibrous flesh, so it is absorbed much more slowly into the system. Fruit also gives a far better flavour to cakes and desserts than granulated sugar, which may be sweet but has no flavour of its own.

Diabetics, indeed all dieters, should also scrutinize labels for added sugar.

Below: Avoid sweetened drinks and opt instead for fizzy water or fresh fruit juice diluted with water.

Sometimes this is easy to avoid – buy fruits canned in fruit juice instead of syrup, for example – but it is not always that clear. Remember that on an ingredients list sucrose, fructose, glucose, maltose, honey, lactose, malt and invert corn syrup are all sugar, under different names.

Sweets and chocolate bars are to be avoided except as a snack before or after sport. Like the fizzy drinks, these not only deliver an instant glucose "hit", but they are very high in calories. If total deprivation is not to be borne, try buying chocolate, for example, in thin tablets or drops. It is amazing how satisfying even a morsel of chocolate can be if you nibble it rather than wolfing down a whole bar!

If an apple does not fill that sweet gap, try a few raisins or fresh dates.

They are just as sweet as a mint or a bar of chocolate but the sugar they contain is embedded in fibre.

Below: To avoid sugar, choose fruits canned in fruit juice, and try apples, fresh dates and raisins as an alternative snack.

REDUCING FATS

Reducing the amount of calories from fat – especially saturated fat – will help greatly in overall weight control and will also fit in with the specifically diabetic diet. Again, it need not be that difficult to achieve: Some of the new low-fat spreads are really very palatable and work excellently in pastry and baking. Does one always need butter or a spread? A ham sandwich with mustard needs neither; a cheese sandwich tastes as good, if not better, with a little low-fat mayonnaise and a lettuce leaf as it does with a thick layer of butter.

Use extra virgin olive oil or sunflower oil, not butter or lard, for cooking – and try not to use even that. Meat and vegetables for stews do not need to be fried at the start of cooking. If they are cooked long and slowly enough, they will have plenty of flavour. If the occasional plate of chips is a must, use the oven-ready ones, which have a substantially lower fat content. Ideally the chips should be abandoned in favour of a baked potato – but a baked potato filled with canned tuna and sweetcorn, or canned salmon

Above: Choose a low-fat filling for baked potatoes: here the potatoes are simply spiced with curry-flavoured onions and served topped with a generous dollop of low-fat natural yogurt.

or baked beans, not with piles of butter or cheese!

Like chips, crisps should really be on the forbidden list. Not only are they calorific and high in fat (even the low-fat ones), but they are very salty – and everyone should be reducing their salt intake! Nuts or (even better) seeds, such as sunflower or pumpkin, maybe lightly salted, are just as good with a drink or as a snack and are very much more nutritious.

USING WHOLEMEAL BREADS AND FLOURS

Even devoted white bread fans, if they persevere with wholemeal breads, will find that although wholemeal breads are not as soft, they have much more flavour. The same applies to using wholemeal flour in baking. The pastry may not be quite as light, but it will be much more flavoursome. There are several other flours that can be used for "lighter but healthier" baking, the most successful of which is gram or chick-pea flour. This is used a lot in Indian cooking. For a diabetic, it has the advantage of being made from a pulse, so it is filled with soluble fibre. Gram flour can be substituted for white flour in most instances and, although the pastry will be a little crumbly, it will taste delicious.

Left: Wholemeal bread is a healthier option than white bread. However, olive-oil breads, such as ciabatta, flavoured with olives or sun-dried tomatoes, are better than highly processed sliced white breads.

FILLING YOURSELF UP

The best way to prevent yourself nibbling – or having the urge to nibble – is by filling yourself up! Try eating large platefuls of colourful salad leaves and raw vegetables, such as tomatoes, peppers, cucumbers, carrots and radishes, or lightly cooked vegetables (most of which, being low in fat and carbohydrate, are on the "eat as much as your like" list for diabetics). For a main meal, bulk out vegetables and salads with cooked wholemeal rice, pasta or cooked beans and pep them up with plenty of chopped fresh herbs and a simple, tasty dressing made from lemon juice and extra virgin olive oil. It is amazing how satisfying they are. Because the food is full of fibre it will take some time for the body to digest, so that feeling of fullness will not have worn off within half an hour as it so often does after over-indulging on sticky cakes.

MONITORING FAT, SODIUM AND FIBRE INTAKES

Diabetics who do not need to lose weight still need to monitor their fat, sodium (salt) and fibre intakes. It is very important that diabetics keep the cholesterol levels in their blood under control to limit the risk of coronary heart disease. They should also keep their blood pressure down. A healthy, low-fat, low-salt, high-fibre diet will do all of these things.

Above: This pilaff of cooked wholemeal rice combined with plenty of lightly cooked vegetables and prawns is a good example of a simple and satisfying – yet low-fat – meal.

TIPS FOR CUTTING CALORIES

• Using a slightly smaller plate so that a smaller portion still looks generous is an old, but very successful, trick!

• Chewing rather than gulping one's food is another. Some experts recommend up to 20 "chews" per mouthful, but even eight or nine will extend the eating period so that the food seems to go further.

• If the weight still refuses to come off, keep a food diary, in which all food consumed is written down.

• Don't con yourself into thinking that you are sticking to a diet, if you forget about the broken biscuit you ate because it fell out of the packet, the chunk of cheese you ate while grating a piece for a recipe, the half sausage the children had left on their plates or the lick of the jam spoon as it went into the washing up.

• Cutting out these few unnecessary calories may be all that it takes for the required amount of weight to be lost.

MODERATION

It is very easy, especially for a newly diagnosed diabetic, to get paranoid about his or her diet. This is not only unnecessary but is positively unhelpful: all this does is raise stress levels, and it is well recognized that stress is more debilitating for a diabetic than for anyone else.

FOODS TO EAT AND FOODS TO AVOID

It is very important for diabetics to keep their overall diet, but the occasional "fall from grace" is not likely to be catastrophic, especially if it can be compensated for at the next meal.

At first it may be hard to remember what is, and is not, allowed, but this will soon become second nature. Comparing calorie values is an easy way to monitor general food intake, but it is even more useful to memorize the following categories of foods as early as possible.

FREE FOODS

These can be eaten whenever and in whatever quantity you want.

- all green and leafy vegetables
- cruciferous vegetables (cauliflower, broccoli, turnip, cabbage, etc)
- salad vegetables (tomatoes, peppers, cucumbers, etc)
- all members of the onion family
- green peas and green beans
- mushrooms
- fruits, such as redcurrants, cranberries and loganberries
- tea, coffee, water, tomato juice (in moderation), clear soups

Left: Eat as much as you like – there's no restriction on the quantity of fresh green beans and peas that diabetics can eat.

Below: Fruits, such as (clockwise from top) pears, grapes, nectarines, raspberries and plums must be counted as part of a diabetic's daily carbohydrate allocation, but make ideal between-meal snacks as well as instant high-fibre desserts.

Above: Salad vegetables, such as fresh tomatoes, cucumbers and a variety of colourful peppers, can be eaten in whatever quantity you want – they are very low in sugar, fat and calories, yet are a good source of micronutrients.

GOOD CARBOHYDRATE/ PROTEIN FOODS

These are good for diabetics to eat, but must be counted as part of an overall carbohydrate and protein allocation.

- all pulses, beans and peas
- brown rice and wholemeal pasta
- oats, wholemeal flours, breads, unsweetened biscuits, etc
- all root vegetables
- all fresh fruits
- all canned fruits as long as canned in fruit juice, not syrup
- dried fruits
- high-fibre unsweetened breakfast cereals
- lean meats or meat products
- fresh and frozen fish
- low-fat cheese, skimmed milk, low-fat yogurts
- all soya products

Right: Soya beans and tofu are good foods for diabetics to eat, however, soya margarine, a healthy alternative to butter, is still a fat and should be used sparingly.

BORDERLINE FOODS

This list reflects less "good" carbohydrate foods and fatty foods – all right to have sometimes in specific quantities but not to over-indulge in.

- white flour, bread, unsweetened biscuits, pastry, rice and pasta
- cornflour, arrowroot, semolina
- unsweetened breakfast cereals
- any fried potato products, such as chips and crisps
- full-fat cheese, cream, full-fat milk, yogurt
- fatty meats, including sausages
- salty meats and fish products
- fruit juices
- reduced-sugar jams, marmalade and other spreads
- alcohol

Left: Borderline foods, such as (clockwise from top) full-fat milk, full-fat, sweetened yogurts, full-fat cheeses and cream, can be eaten occasionally, but don't over-indulge!

BAD FOODS

These are to be avoided whenever possible and, when eaten, only to be consumed in very small quantities.

- sugar: caster, granulated, demerara; also honey and golden syrup
- sweets, such as candies, chocolate
- full-sugar chewing gum
- full-sugar jams, marmalades and similar spreads
- sweet biscuits, cakes and buns made with white flour and sugar
- desserts made with refined flours and refined sugar

- fruit canned in syrup
- ice cream and ice lollies
- fruit squashes, sweetened drinks, sweetened fizzy drinks and colas
- sweetened breakfast cereals

Below: No longer banned entirely, but sweet treats, such as (clockwise from top left) golden syrup, caster sugar, honey, icing sugar and demerara sugar, should only be eaten in very small quantities.

Above: Chocolate biscuits, cakes and buns are best avoided by diabetics.

ALCOHOL

Alcohol, such as red wine and lager (*right*), is not entirely off limits for diabetics but must be taken in moderation and calculated into the diet. Beware of low-alcohol drinks. Because less of the sugar has been converted to alcohol, they may contain more sugar. Conversely, low-sugar drinks may contain more alcohol! Remember that alcohol is calorific; if you are trying to lose weight, keep your consumption low. It is also important to remember that excess alcohol consumption puts a strain on the liver and the pancreas – both organs that are already under pressure in a diabetic.

ABOUT THE RECIPES

We hope that the recipes in this collection will give diabetics (and non-diabetics) ideas for other dishes that will fulfil the diabetic diet criteria. Any good cookery book should encourage experimentation, so feel free to change – or indeed improve the recipes that follow.

Our aim has been to introduce ingredients high in soluble fibre, such as pulses and beans and low in fats and sugars, combined with other more familiar ingredients.

Many of the main course dishes add lentils or dried beans to meat and vegetables. The only oil in savoury dishes is olive oil or sunflower oil. All baking is done with low-fat spreads and natural fruit sweeteners (apart from the occasional chocolate treat). Those who have never cooked with dried or fresh fruit purées will be amazed how good the results are – and how little they miss the sugar.

Sodium Levels – Regular stock cubes can be very high in salt, so look out for "natural" or "organic" stock cubes with no added salt. Whenever possible, buy "no added salt or sugar" canned beans and vegetables.

STARTERS AND SOUPS

Vegetable starters and soups are ideal for diabetics as they are often low in fat and sugar and high in fibre. What is more, it is easy to make them appealing to the whole family. This colourful and tasty collection includes a delectable salad made with avocados and strawberries, tender courgettes stuffed with a piquant tomato and herb salsa, and a range of stunning soups made with vibrant vegetables and pulses.

Chilled Stuffed Courgettes

Full of flavour but low in calories and fat, this superb starter is also ideal as a light lunch dish.

INGREDIENTS

Serves 6
6 courgettes
1 Spanish onion, very finely chopped
1 garlic clove, crushed
60–90ml/4–6 tbsp well-flavoured
  French dressing
1 green pepper
3 tomatoes, peeled and seeded
15ml/1 tbsp rinsed capers
5ml/1 tsp chopped fresh parsley
5ml/1 tsp chopped fresh basil
sea salt and ground black pepper
parsley sprigs, to garnish

1 Top and tail the courgettes, but do not peel them. Bring a large shallow pan of lightly salted water to the boil, add the courgettes and simmer for 2–3 minutes until they are lightly cooked. Drain well.

2 Cut the courgettes in half lengthways. Carefully scoop out the flesh, leaving the courgette shells intact, and chop the flesh into small cubes. Place in a bowl and cover with half the chopped onion. Dot with the crushed garlic. Drizzle 30ml/2 tbsp of the dressing over, cover and marinate for 2–3 hours. Wrap the courgette shells tightly in clear film, and chill them until they are required.

3 Cut the pepper in half and remove the core and seeds. Dice the flesh. Chop the tomatoes and capers finely. Stir the pepper, tomatoes and capers into the courgette mixture, with the remaining onion and the chopped herbs. Season with salt and pepper. Pour over enough of the remaining dressing to moisten the mixture and toss well. Spoon the filling into the courgette shells, arrange on a platter and serve garnished with parsley.

NUTRITION NOTES	
Per portion:	
Energy	95kcals/390kJ
Fat, total	7.3g
saturated fat	1.1g
polyunsaturated fat	0.9g
monounsaturated fat	4.9g
Carbohydrate	5.3g
sugar, total	4.75g
starch	0.2g
Fibre – NSP	1.95g
Sodium	60mg

Persian Omelette

Serve this spiced omelette hot or cold, in wedges as a starter, or cut it into bite-size pieces for serving with drinks. The herbs and nuts add texture and taste.

INGREDIENTS

Serves 8

30ml/2 tbsp olive oil or sunflower oil
2 leeks, finely chopped
350g/12oz fresh spinach, washed and chopped, or 150g/5oz thawed frozen chopped spinach, drained
12 eggs
8 spring onions, finely chopped
2 handfuls fresh parsley, finely chopped
1–2 handfuls fresh coriander, chopped
2 fresh tarragon sprigs, chopped, or 2.5ml/½ tsp dried tarragon
handful of fresh chives, chopped
1 small fresh dill sprig, chopped, or 1.5ml/¼ tsp dried dill
2–4 fresh mint sprigs, chopped
40g/1½ oz/⅓ cup walnuts or pecan nuts, chopped
40g/1½ oz/½ cup pine nuts
sea salt and ground black pepper
salad, to serve

1 Heat the oil in a large shallow pan that can be used under the grill. Add the leeks and fry them gently for about 5 minutes until they are just beginning to soften.

2 If using fresh spinach, add it to the pan containing the leeks and cook for 2–3 minutes over a medium heat until the spinach has just wilted.

3 Beat the eggs in a bowl with a fork. Add the leek and spinach mixture (or the leeks with the thawed frozen spinach), then stir in the spring onions, with all the herbs and nuts. Season with salt and pepper. Pour the mixture into the pan and cover with a lid or foil.

4 Cook over a very gentle heat for 25 minutes or until set. Remove the lid and brown the top under a hot grill. Serve, with salad.

NUTRITION NOTES	
Per portion:	
Energy	258kcals/1073kJ
Fat, total	21g
saturated fat	3.9g
polyunsaturated fat	6.1g
monounsaturated fat	8.7g
Carbohydrate	2.8g
sugar, total	2.3g
starch	0.15g
Fibre – NSP	1.9g
Sodium	192mg

Aubergine and Smoked Trout Pâté

INGREDIENTS

Serves 6
1 large aubergine
2–3 garlic cloves, unpeeled
4 smoked trout fillets
juice of 1 lemon
sea salt and ground black pepper
toast, to serve

NUTRITION NOTES

Per portion:

Energy	145kcals/609kJ
Fat, total	4.7g
saturated fat	1.05g
polyunsaturated fat	1.6g
monounsaturated fat	1.6g
Carbohydrate	1.6g
sugar, total	1.1g
starch	0.5g
Fibre – NSP	1.1g
Sodium	89mg

1 Slice the aubergine thickly and spread out the slices in a steamer. Tuck the whole garlic cloves among the slices. Steam over boiling water for 10–15 minutes until both the aubergine slices and the garlic cloves are quite soft.

2 Carefully cut the skins from around the aubergine slices using a small sharp knife.

3 Skin the trout fillets and chop them roughly. Put them in a food processor. Pop the garlic flesh out of the skins and add it to the processor with the aubergine slices. Add the lemon juice and process until smooth. Spoon into a bowl and season. Cool, then chill. Serve with toast.

Avocado and Strawberry Salad

The combination of avocado and strawberries works surprisingly well in this refreshing salad.

INGREDIENTS

Serves 6
2 large, ripe avocados
juice of 2–3 lemons
15 strawberries
120ml/4fl oz/½ cup low-fat
   natural yogurt
15–30 ml/1–2 tbsp chopped fresh mint
sea salt and ground black pepper
sprig of mint, to garnish

COOK'S TIP

Serve the salad straightaway, before the avocado slices have a chance to discolour.

1 Cut the avocados in half and remove the skin and stones. Cut the avocado flesh into thin slices, then place the slices in a bowl and sprinkle over half the lemon juice.

NUTRITION NOTES

Per portion:

Energy	93kcals/387kJ
Fat, total	8g
saturated fat	1.75g
polyunsaturated fat	0.9g
monounsaturated fat	4.9g
Carbohydrate	3.5g
sugar, total	2.8g
starch	0g
Fibre – NSP	1.5g
Sodium	20mg

2 Halve or slice the strawberries and toss them lightly with the avocado slices in the bowl. Mix the yogurt with enough cold water to give a pouring consistency. Stir in the mint and season to taste. Spoon the dressing over the salad, garnish with mint and serve.

Sweet Potato and Red Pepper Soup

As colourful as it is good to eat, this soup is a sure winner.

INGREDIENTS

Serves 6

500g/1¼ lb sweet potato
2 red peppers, about 225g/8oz, seeded
   and cubed
1 onion, roughly chopped
2 large garlic cloves, roughly chopped
300ml/ ½ pint/1¼ cups dry white wine
1.2 litres/2 pints/5 cups vegetable or
   light chicken stock
Tabasco sauce (optional)
sea salt and ground black pepper
country bread, to serve

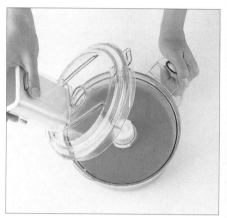

1 Peel the sweet potato and cut it into cubes. Put these in a saucepan with the red peppers, onion, garlic, wine and vegetable or chicken stock. Bring to the boil, lower the heat and simmer for 30 minutes or until all the vegetables are quite soft.

2 Transfer the mixture to a blender or food processor and process until smooth. Season to taste with salt, pepper and a generous dash of Tabasco, if liked. Pour into a tureen or serving bowl and cool slightly. Serve warm or at room temperature, with bread.

------ COOK'S TIP ------

Garnish the soup with finely diced red, green or yellow pepper, if you like.

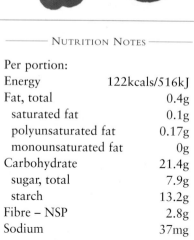

------ NUTRITION NOTES ------

Per portion:

Energy	122kcals/516kJ
Fat, total	0.4g
saturated fat	0.1g
polyunsaturated fat	0.17g
monounsaturated fat	0g
Carbohydrate	21.4g
sugar, total	7.9g
starch	13.2g
Fibre – NSP	2.8g
Sodium	37mg

Garlicky Lentil Soup

High in fibre, lentils make a very tasty soup. Unlike many pulses, they do not need to be soaked before being cooked.

INGREDIENTS

Serves 6

225g/8oz/1 cup red lentils, rinsed
  and drained
2 onions, finely chopped
2 large garlic cloves, finely chopped
1 carrot, very finely chopped
30ml/2 tbsp olive oil
2 bay leaves
generous pinch of dried marjoram
  or oregano
1.5 litres/2½ pints/6¼ cups vegetable
  stock
30ml/2 tbsp red wine vinegar
sea salt and ground black pepper
celery leaves, to garnish
crusty rolls, to serve

COOK'S TIP

If you buy your lentils loose, remember to tip them into a sieve or colander and pick them over, removing any pieces of grit, before rinsing them.

1 Put all the ingredients except the vinegar, garnish and seasoning in a large heavy-based saucepan. Bring to the boil over a medium heat, then lower the heat and simmer for 1½ hours, stirring the soup occasionally to prevent the lentils from sticking to the bottom of the pan.

2 Remove the bay leaves and add the red wine vinegar, with salt and pepper to taste. If the soup is too thick, thin it with a little extra vegetable stock or water. Serve the soup in heated bowls, garnished with celery leaves and accompanied by crusty rolls.

NUTRITION NOTES

Per portion:

Energy	167kcals/748kJ
Fat, total	5.6g
saturated fat	0.8g
polyunsaturated fat	0.65g
monounsaturated fat	3.7g
Carbohydrate	23.6g
sugar, total	2.6g
starch	19.3g
Fibre – NSP	2.45g
Sodium	18.5mg

Mrs Blencowe's Green Pea Soup with Spinach

This lovely green soup was invented by the wife of a seventeenth-century British Member of Parliament, and it has stood the test of time.

INGREDIENTS

Serves 6

450g/1lb/generous 3 cups podded fresh
   or frozen peas
1 leek, finely sliced
2 garlic cloves, crushed
2 rindless back bacon slices,
   finely diced
1.2 litres/2 pints/5 cups ham or
   chicken stock
30ml/2 tbsp olive oil
50g/2oz fresh spinach, shredded
40g/1½ oz white cabbage, very
   finely shredded
½ small lettuce, very finely shredded
1 celery stick, finely chopped
large handful of parsley, finely chopped
½ carton mustard and cress
20ml/4 tsp chopped fresh mint
pinch of mace
sea salt and ground black pepper

1 Put the peas, leek, garlic and bacon in a large saucepan. Add the stock, bring to the boil, then lower the heat and simmer for 20 minutes.

2 About 5 minutes before the pea mixture is ready, heat the oil in a deep frying pan.

COOK'S TIP

Use 25g/1oz frozen leaf spinach if fresh spinach is not available.

3 Add the spinach, cabbage, lettuce, celery and herbs. Cover and sweat the mixture over a low heat until soft.

4 Transfer the pea mixture to a blender or food processor; process until smooth. Return to the clean saucepan, add the sweated vegetables and herbs and heat through. Season with mace, salt and pepper and serve.

NUTRITION NOTES

Per portion:

Energy	140kcals/575kJ
Fat, total	7.6g
saturated fat	1.45g
polyunsaturated fat	1.2g
monounsaturated fat	4.4g
Carbohydrate	10g
sugar, total	2.7g
starch	5.8g
Fibre – NSP	4.4g
Sodium	165mg

Cream of Celeriac and Spinach Soup

Celeriac has a wonderful flavour that is reminiscent of celery, but also adds a slightly nutty taste. Here it is combined with spinach to make a delicious soup.

INGREDIENTS

Serves 6

1 leek
500g/1¼lb celeriac
1 litre/1¾ pints/4 cups water
250ml/8fl oz/1 cup dry white wine
200g/7oz fresh spinach leaves
semi-skimmed milk (optional)
25g/1oz/⅓ cup pine nuts
sea salt, ground black pepper and
   grated nutmeg

1 Trim and slit the leek. Rinse it under running water to remove any grit, then slice it thickly. Peel the celeriac and dice the flesh.

2 Mix the water and wine in a jug. Place the leek and celeriac, with the spinach, in a deep saucepan and pour over the liquid. Bring to the boil, lower the heat and simmer for 10–15 minutes, until the vegetables are soft.

3 Purée the celeriac mixture, in batches if necessary, in a blender or food processor. Return to the clean pan and season to taste with salt, pepper and nutmeg. If the soup is too thick, thin it with a little water or semi-skimmed milk. Reheat gently.

4 Roast the pine nuts in a dry non-stick frying pan until golden. Sprinkle them over the soup and serve.

NUTRITION NOTES	
Per portion:	
Energy	82kcals/340kJ
Fat, total	3.5g
saturated fat	0.25g
polyunsaturated fat	1.9g
monounsaturated fat	0.85g
Carbohydrate	3.25g
sugar, total	2.7g
starch	0.5g
Fibre – NSP	4g
Sodium	124mg

FISH AND MEAT

Fish is excellent food for diabetics, and
such dishes as a pilaff with spicy
prawns, or parcels of filo pastry filled
with sardines, are both healthy and
light. Meat dishes, which need to be
high in fibre for diabetics, tend to be
heartier fare. The selection here includes
beef and lentil balls cooked in a tomato
sauce, leg of lamb roasted until tender
with flageolet beans, and sausages
combined with mixed beans and bacon
to make a warming casserole.

Fennel and Smoked Haddock Chowder

This soup is substantial enough to serve as a main meal with plenty of poppy seed bread.

INGREDIENTS

Serves 8
1 large fennel bulb
2 large leeks, very finely sliced
225g/8oz new potatoes, scrubbed, halved or quartered if large
5ml/1 tsp dill seed
2 large garlic cloves, thinly sliced
½ lemon
1.5 litres/2½ pints/6¼ cups water
300ml/½ pint/1¼ cups dry white wine
225g/8oz smoked haddock fillet, skinned
sea salt and ground black pepper
chopped fresh parsley, to garnish

1 Quarter the fennel, cut away the core and slice each piece very finely. Place in a saucepan with the leeks, potatoes, dill seed and garlic. Cut the half lemon into thick slices and add these to the pan. Pour the water and wine into the pan.

2 Season with plenty of pepper, then bring to the boil, lower the heat and simmer for about 30 minutes or until the potatoes and fennel are both cooked through.

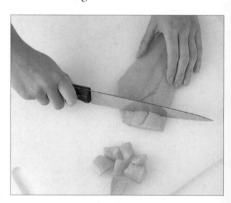

3 Cut the haddock into chunks, add to the pan and simmer the mixture for 10 minutes more. Remove the lemon slices. Stir the soup gently. Add salt and pepper to taste. Sprinkle with parsley and serve.

— NUTRITION NOTES —	
Per portion:	
Energy	75kcals/316kJ
Fat, total	0.5g
saturated fat	0.1g
polyunsaturated fat	0.15g
monounsaturated fat	0.1g
Carbohydrate	6g
sugar, total	1.5g
starch	4.35g
Fibre – NSP	1.2g
Sodium	221mg

Linguine with Smoked Salmon

INGREDIENTS

Serves 6

30ml/2 tbsp olive oil
115g/4oz/1 cup button mushrooms, finely sliced
250ml/8fl oz/1 cup dry white wine
7.5ml/1½ tsp fresh dill or 5ml/1 tsp dried dill weed
handful of fresh chives, snipped
300ml/½ pint/1¼ cups very low-fat unsweetened soya cream or very low-fat fromage frais
225g/8oz smoked salmon, cut into thin strips
lemon juice
350g/12oz fresh linguine or spaghetti
sea salt and ground black pepper
whole chives, to garnish

1 Heat the oil in a wide, shallow saucepan. Add the finely sliced mushrooms and fry them over a gentle heat for 4–5 minutes until they are softened but not coloured.

2 Pour the white wine into the pan. Increase the heat and boil rapidly for about 5 minutes, until the wine has reduced considerably.

3 Stir in the herbs and the soya cream or fromage frais. Fold in the salmon and reheat gently, but do not let the sauce boil or it will curdle. Stir in pepper and lemon juice to taste. Cover the pan and keep the sauce warm.

4 Cook the pasta in a large saucepan of lightly salted boiling water until just tender. Drain, rinse thoroughly in boiling water and drain again. Turn into a warmed serving dish and toss gently with the salmon sauce before serving, garnished with chives.

NUTRITION NOTES

Per portion:

Energy	346kcals/1464kJ
Fat, total	8.3g
saturated fat	1.35g
polyunsaturated fat	1.6g
monounsaturated fat	4.5g
Carbohydrate	42.4g
sugar, total	5.8g
starch	36.5g
Fibre – NSP	5.16g
Sodium	800mg

COOK'S TIP

Soya cream may be an acquired taste, but it is a very successful low-fat substitute for dairy cream in dishes like this one, with a strong flavour of their own.

Sardine and Spinach Parcels

If you needed encouragement to eat more oily fish, this recipe will provide the perfect excuse.

Ingredients

Serves 6

2 x 120g/4¼oz cans large sardines in oil
3 leeks, finely chopped
300g/11oz fresh spinach leaves,
    finely shredded
2 tomatoes, peeled, seeded and
    finely chopped
lemon juice
24 sheets of filo pastry, about 20cm/8in
    square, thawed if frozen
30ml/2 tbsp olive oil, for brushing filo
sea salt and ground black pepper
salad leaves, to garnish

1 Preheat the oven to 180°C/350°F/ Gas 4. Drain the oil from one of the cans of sardines into a frying pan. Set six sardines aside. Heat the oil and fry the leeks for 5 minutes. Add the spinach and tomatoes and cook over a low heat for 5 minutes until soft. Add salt, pepper and lemon juice to taste.

2 Stack four sheets of filo, brushing each sheet with olive oil and laying each sheet at an angle of 45° to the one below. Spoon a sixth of the vegetable mixture into the centre of the top sheet. Press a sardine into the middle of the vegetable mixture.

3 Fold over the filo to make a parcel, brushing each fold with olive oil. Brush the top of the parcel with oil and place it on a baking sheet. Make five more parcels. Bake the filo parcels for 20 minutes, or until the filo is crisp and brown. Garnish with salad leaves.

Nutrition Notes	
Per portion:	
Energy	251kcals/1048kJ
Fat, total	12g
saturated fat	1.9g
polyunsaturated fat	2.8g
monounsaturated fat	5.65g
Carbohydrate	22.5g
sugar, total	2.5g
starch	20g
Fibre – NSP	2.2g
Sodium	253mg

Turkish Prawn Pilaff

INGREDIENTS

Serves 6

60ml/4 tbsp olive oil
1 onion, finely chopped
2 large red peppers, seeded and finely
 chopped
2 garlic cloves, finely chopped
350g/12oz/1½ cups brown rice
5ml/1 tsp ground allspice
5ml/1 tsp ground cumin
10ml/2 tsp dried mint or basil
225g/8oz cooked peeled prawns,
 thawed if frozen
45ml/3 tbsp currants
juice of 2 large lemons
2 handfuls fresh parsley, finely chopped
sea salt and ground black pepper
salad, to serve

1 Heat the oil in a shallow saucepan. Fry the onion, peppers and garlic over a low heat for 10 minutes until the onion has softened but not browned.

NUTRITION NOTES

Per portion:	
Energy	383kcals/1612kJ
Fat, total	12.6g
saturated fat	2g
polyunsaturated fat	1.7g
monounsaturated fat	7.9g
Carbohydrate	58g
sugar, total	10g
starch	47g
Fibre – NSP	2.4g
Sodium	606mg

2 Add the rice, spices and mint or basil. Stir over the heat for 2–3 minutes, then add enough water to cover the rice. Bring to the boil, lower the heat and simmer, uncovered, for 10–15 minutes or until the rice is just tender, but still has a little bite to it.

3 Add the prawns, currants and a little salt, to taste. Cook for about 4 minutes more, until the prawns have heated through, then add the lemon juice and chopped parsley. Add pepper to taste. Serve the pilaff warm or cold, with salad.

Spiced Topside of Beef

A spicy marinade gives the beef a wonderful flavour, while slow cooking keeps it very moist.

INGREDIENTS

Serves 8

10ml/2 tsp coriander seeds
5ml/1 tsp each aniseeds, fennel seeds, dried thyme, ground cloves, sea salt and ground black pepper
2.5ml/½ tsp ground cinnamon
600ml/1 pint/2½ cups dry white wine
1–1.2kg/2¼–2½lb topside of beef
30ml/2 tbsp olive oil
2 onions, finely chopped
2 carrots, finely chopped
2 celery sticks, finely chopped
1 parsnip, finely chopped
4 French beans, finely chopped
8 mushrooms, finely chopped
300ml/½ pint/1¼ cups home-made jellied beef stock or chicken stock
105ml/7 tbsp red wine
2 fresh parsley sprigs
baked potatoes, to serve

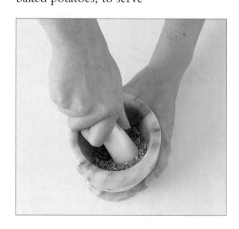

1 Put the seeds in a mortar and pound them with a pestle. Stir in the rest of the spices and seasonings, then tip the mixture into a bowl and stir in the white wine.

---- COOK'S TIP ----

Patience is the secret of this superb casserole. Marinate the meat for the time stated, and cook it very slowly.

2 Put the beef in a deep glass or china bowl. Pour the spicy marinade over the beef, cover the bowl and leave to marinate in the fridge or a cool larder for about 24 hours.

3 Preheat the oven to 150°C/300°F/Gas 2. Heat the oil in a deep casserole just large enough to hold the beef snugly. Add all the vegetables and cook over a gentle heat for 15–20 minutes or until they start to soften.

4 Lift the beef out of the marinade and place on top of the vegetables. Strain 300ml/½ pint/1¼ cups of the marinade into a jug and add the stock and red wine.

5 Pour the liquid over the beef. Add the parsley, cover and place in the oven. Bake for 2–3 hours or until the beef is tender. Serve with potatoes.

──── NUTRITION NOTES ────	
Per portion:	
Energy	260kcals/1088kJ
Fat, total	7.95g
saturated fat	2g
polyunsaturated fat	0.73g
monounsaturated fat	4.25g
Carbohydrate	4.3g
sugar, total	2.8g
starch	0.8g
Fibre – NSP	1.25g
Sodium	203mg

Lamb with Flageolets and Green Peppercorns

Roasting the lamb slowly on a bed of beans results in a dish that combines meltingly tender meat with plenty of soluble fibre.

INGREDIENTS

Serves 6

8–10 garlic cloves, peeled
1.75kg/4–4½lb leg of lamb
30ml/2 tbsp olive oil
400g/14oz fresh spinach leaves
400g/14oz can flageolet beans, drained
400g/14oz can butter beans, drained
2 large fresh rosemary sprigs
15–30ml/1–2 tbsp drained green
    peppercorns
potatoes, to serve

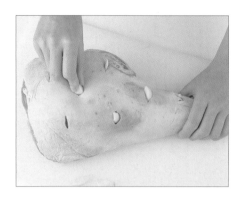

1 Preheat the oven to 150°C/300°F/ Gas 2. Set 4 garlic cloves aside and slice the rest lengthways into three or four pieces. Make shallow slits in the skin of the lamb and insert a piece of garlic in each.

2 Heat the oil in a roasting tin or a heavy flameproof casserole that is large enough to hold the lamb. Add the reserved garlic and the spinach and cook briskly for 4–5 minutes or until the spinach is wilted.

3 Add the flageolets and butter beans and tuck the rosemary sprigs and peppercorns among them. Place the lamb on top. Cover with foil or a lid. Roast the lamb for 3–4 hours until it is cooked to your taste. Serve with the spinach and beans and potatoes.

NUTRITION NOTES	
Per portion:	
Energy	312kcals/1306kJ
Fat, total	14.5g
saturated fat	4.6g
polyunsaturated fat	1.4g
monounsaturated fat	6.9g
Carbohydrate	17.8g
sugar, total	2.3g
starch	14.2g
Fibre – NSP	6g
Sodium	172mg

Smoked Bacon, Sausage and Bean Casserole

This casserole is the perfect choice for a winter's evening.

INGREDIENTS

Serves 6

150g/5oz/⅔ cup each dried black-
    eyed, pinto and cannellini beans
15ml/1 tbsp olive oil
6 rindless smoked streaky bacon rashers
6 large country pork sausages
3 large carrots, halved
3 large onions, halved
1 small garlic bulb, separated
    into cloves
4 bay leaves
2 fresh thyme sprigs
15–30ml/1–2 tbsp dried green
    peppercorns
300ml/½ pint/1¼ cups unsalted
    vegetable stock or water
300ml/½ pint/1¼ cups red wine
sea salt and ground black pepper
green salad, to serve
thyme sprigs, to garnish

1 Bring a large saucepan of unsalted water to the boil. Add the beans and boil vigorously for 30 minutes. Drain and set aside.

NUTRITION NOTES

Per portion:

Energy	410kcals/1714kJ
Fat, total	20.5g
saturated fat	6.7g
polyunsaturated fat	2.3g
monounsaturated fat	10.25g
Carbohydrate	33.8g
sugar, total	5.4g
starch	25.6g
Fibre – NSP	7g
Sodium	467mg

2 Pour the olive oil into a large heavy-based flameproof casserole, then lay the bacon rashers on top. Add the whole sausages and the halved carrots and onions. Peel but do not slice the garlic cloves, then press them into the mixture with the bay leaves, thyme sprigs and dried peppercorns. Spoon the cooked, drained beans over the top of the mixture.

3 Pour in the stock or water and wine. Cover the casserole and bring the liquid to the boil over a medium heat. Reduce the heat to the lowest setting and cook for 4–6 hours, stirring periodically and topping up the liquid if necessary. Stir the mixture and season before serving, garnished with thyme. Serve from the casserole, accompanied by a green salad.

Two-way Chicken with Vegetables

This tender slow-cooked chicken makes a tasty lunch or supper, with the stock and remaining vegetables providing a nourishing soup as a second meal!

INGREDIENTS

Serves 6

1.5kg/3lb chicken
2 onions, quartered
3 carrots, thickly sliced
2 celery sticks, chopped
1 parsnip or turnip, thickly sliced
50g/2oz/½ cup button mushrooms, with stalks, roughly chopped
1–2 fresh thyme sprigs or 5ml/1 tsp dried thyme
4 bay leaves
large bunch of fresh parsley
115g/4oz/1 cup wholemeal pasta shapes
sea salt and ground black pepper
new potatoes or pasta, mangetouts or French beans and bread, to serve

1 Trim the chicken of any extra fat. Put it in a flameproof casserole and add the vegetables and herbs. Pour in water to cover. Bring to the boil over a medium heat, skimming off any scum. When the water boils, lower the heat and simmer for 2–3 hours. Carve the meat neatly, discarding the skin and bones, but returning any small pieces to the pan. Serve the chicken with some of the vegetables from the pan, plus new potatoes or pasta and mangetouts or French beans, if you like.

2 Remove any large pieces of parsley and thyme from the pan, let the remaining mixture cool, then chill it overnight. Next day, lift off the fat that has solidified on the surface. Reheat the soup gently.

3 When the soup comes to the boil, add the pasta shapes, with salt, if required, and cook for 10–12 minutes or until the pasta is tender. Season with salt and pepper and garnish with parsley. Serve with wholemeal bread.

NUTRITION NOTES	
Per portion:	
Energy	212kcals/896kJ
Fat, total	3.3g
saturated fat	0.8g
polyunsaturated fat	0.8g
monounsaturated fat	1.3g
Carbohydrate	17.5g
sugar, total	3.7g
starch	12.7g
Fibre – NSP	3.15g
Sodium	130mg

Chicken Baked with Butter Beans and Garlic

A one-pot meal that combines chicken with leeks, fennel and garlic-flavoured butter beans.

INGREDIENTS

Serves 6

2 leeks
1 small fennel bulb, roughly chopped
4 garlic cloves, peeled
2 x 400g/14oz cans butter
  beans, drained
2 large handfuls fresh parsley, chopped
300ml/½ pint/1¼ cups dry white wine
300ml/½ pint/1¼ cups vegetable stock
1.5kg/3lb chicken
parsley sprigs, to garnish
cooked green vegetables, to serve

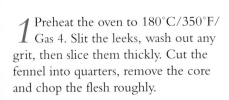

1 Preheat the oven to 180°C/350°F/Gas 4. Slit the leeks, wash out any grit, then slice them thickly. Cut the fennel into quarters, remove the core and chop the flesh roughly.

NUTRITION NOTES	
Per portion:	
Energy	304kcals/1288kJ
Fat, total	3.4g
saturated fat	0.8g
polyunsaturated fat	0.9g
monounsaturated fat	1.2g
Carbohydrate	26.2g
sugar, total	3.2g
starch	21.2g
Fibre – NSP	8g
Sodium	105mg

2 Mix the leeks, fennel, whole garlic cloves, butter beans and parsley in a bowl. Spread out the mixture on the bottom of a heavy-based flameproof casserole that is large enough to hold the chicken. Pour in the white wine and vegetable stock.

3 Place the chicken on top. Bring to the boil, cover the casserole and transfer it to the oven. Bake for 1–1½ hours, until the chicken is cooked and so tender that it falls off the bone. Garnish with parsley and serve with lightly cooked green vegetables.

Beef and Lentil Balls with Tomato Sauce

Mixing lentils with the minced beef not only boosts the fibre content of these meatballs but also adds to the flavour.

INGREDIENTS

Serves 8

15ml/1 tbsp olive oil
2 onions, finely chopped
2 celery sticks, finely chopped
2 large carrots, finely chopped
400g/14oz lean minced beef
200g/7oz/scant 1 cup brown lentils
400g/14oz can plum tomatoes
30ml/2 tbsp tomato purée
2 bay leaves
300ml/½ pint/1¼ cups vegetable stock
175ml/6fl oz/¾ cup red wine
30–45ml/2–3 tbsp Worcestershire sauce
2 eggs
2 large handfuls of fresh parsley, chopped
sea salt and ground black pepper
riced potatoes and green salad, to serve

For the tomato sauce

4 onions, finely chopped
2 x 400g/14oz cans chopped tomatoes
60ml/4 tbsp dry red wine
3 fresh dill sprigs, finely chopped

1 Start by making the tomato sauce. Combine the onions, canned plum tomatoes and red wine in a saucepan. Bring to the boil, lower the heat, cover the pan and simmer for 30 minutes. Purée the mixture in a blender or food processor, then return it to the clean saucepan and set it aside.

2 Make the meatballs. Heat the oil in a large heavy-based saucepan and cook the chopped onions, celery and carrots for 5–10 minutes or until the onions and carrots have softened.

3 Add the minced beef and cook over a high heat, stirring frequently, until the meat is lightly browned.

4 Add the lentils, tomatoes, tomato purée, bay leaves, vegetable stock and wine. Mix well and bring to the boil. Lower the heat and simmer for 20–30 minutes until the liquid has been absorbed. Remove the bay leaves, then stir the Worcestershire sauce into the lentil mixture.

5 Remove the pan from the heat and add the eggs and parsley. Season with salt and pepper and mix well, then leave to cool. Meanwhile, preheat the oven to 180°C/350°F/Gas 4.

6 Shape the beef mixture into neat balls, rolling them in your hands. Arrange in an ovenproof dish and bake for 25 minutes. While the meatballs are baking, reheat the tomato sauce. Just before serving, stir in the chopped dill. Pour the tomato sauce over the meatballs and serve. Riced potatoes and salad make excellent accompaniments.

NUTRITION NOTES	
Per portion:	
Energy	272kcals/1154kJ
Fat, total	9.3g
saturated fat	2.9g
polyunsaturated fat	0.8g
monounsaturated fat	4.2g
Carbohydrate	22.65g
sugar, total	9g
starch	11.5g
Fibre – NSP	4.5g
Sodium	155mg

VEGETABLES AND VEGETARIAN DISHES

The increasing popularity of vegetarian food is good news for diabetics. Dishes, such as a casserole of red cabbage and apple, or baked vegetables with artichokes, can be served as main meals, or in smaller portions as accompaniments to meat or fish dishes. Others, such as a risotto made with red peppers and a flan of mushrooms and sunflower seeds, make excellent meals on their own, with a salad or served with another vegetable.

Red Cabbage and Apple Casserole

The brilliant colour and pungent flavour make this an excellent winter dish. Serve it solo, with plenty of rye bread, or as a vegetable accompaniment.

INGREDIENTS

Serves 6

3 onions, chopped
2 fennel bulbs, roughly chopped
675g/1½lb red cabbage, shredded
30ml/2 tbsp caraway seeds
3 large tart eating apples or 1 large
  cooking apple
6 rindless streaky bacon rashers
  (optional)
300ml/½ pint/1¼ cups low-fat
  natural yogurt
15ml/1 tbsp creamed horseradish sauce
sea salt and ground black pepper

1 Preheat the oven to 150°C/300°F/ Gas 2. Mix the onions, fennel, red cabbage and caraway seeds in a bowl. Peel and chop the apples and the bacon rashers, if using, then stir them into the cabbage mixture. Transfer to a casserole. Mix the yogurt with the creamed horseradish sauce.

2 Stir the yogurt and horseradish mixture into the casserole, season with salt and pepper and cover tightly. Bake for 1½ hours, stirring once or twice. Serve hot.

— NUTRITION NOTES —	
Per portion (with bacon):	
Energy	158kcals/660kJ
Fat, total	9.7g
saturated fat	3.4g
polyunsaturated fat	1.4g
monounsaturated fat	4.05g
Carbohydrate	12.8g
sugar, total	11.6g
starch	0.2g
Fibre – NSP	4g
Sodium	378mg

Mixed Vegetables with Artichokes

Baking a vegetable medley in the oven is a wonderfully easy way of producing a quick and simple, wholesome mid-week meal.

INGREDIENTS

Serves 4

30ml/2 tbsp olive oil
675g/1½lb frozen broad beans
4 turnips, peeled and sliced
4 leeks, sliced
1 red pepper, seeded and sliced
200g/7oz fresh spinach leaves or
  115g/4oz frozen spinach
2 x 400g/14oz cans artichoke
  hearts, drained
60ml/4 tbsp pumpkin seeds
soy sauce
sea salt and ground black pepper
rice, baked potatoes or wholemeal
  bread, to serve

1 Preheat the oven to 180°C/350°F/ Gas 4. Pour the oil into a casserole. Cook the broad beans in a saucepan of boiling lightly salted water for about 10 minutes. Drain the beans and place them with the turnips, leeks, red pepper slices, spinach and canned artichoke hearts in the casserole.

2 Cover the casserole and bake the vegetables for 30–40 minutes, or until the turnips are soft.

3 Stir in the pumpkin seeds and soy sauce to taste. Season with ground black pepper. Serve solo or with rice sprinkled with chopped fresh herbs, baked potatoes or bread.

— NUTRITION NOTES —	
Per portion:	
Energy	335kcals/1410kJ
Fat, total	13.4g
saturated fat	2.2g
polyunsaturated fat	3.3g
monounsaturated fat	6.5g
Carbohydrate	34.95g
sugar, total	11.4g
starch	19.4g
Fibre – NSP	16.3g
Sodium	151.5mg

Purée of Lentils with Baked Eggs

This unusual dish makes an excellent vegetarian supper. If you prefer, bake the purée and eggs in one large baking dish.

INGREDIENTS

Serves 6
450g/1lb/2 cups red lentils
3 leeks, thinly sliced
10ml/2 tsp coriander seeds,
  finely crushed
15ml/1 tbsp chopped fresh coriander
30ml/2 tbsp chopped fresh mint
15ml/1 tbsp red wine vinegar
1 litre/1¾ pints/4 cups vegetable stock
4 eggs
sea salt and ground black pepper
generous handful of fresh
  parsley, chopped, to garnish

1 Put the lentils in a deep saucepan. Add the leeks, coriander seeds, fresh coriander, mint, vinegar and stock. Bring to the boil, then lower the heat and simmer for 30–40 minutes or until the lentils are cooked and have absorbed all the liquid.

2 Preheat the oven to 180°C/350°F/ Gas 4. Season the lentils with salt and pepper and mix well. Spread out in four lightly greased baking dishes.

3 Using the back of a spoon, make a hollow in the lentil mixture in each dish. Break an egg into each hollow. Cover the dishes with foil and bake for 15–20 minutes or until the eggs are set. Sprinkle with plenty of chopped parsley and serve at once.

NUTRITION NOTES

Per portion:	
Energy	470kcals/1985kJ
Fat, total	9.1g
saturated fat	2.2g
polyunsaturated fat	1.5g
monounsaturated fat	3.38g
Carbohydrate	65.8g
sugar, total	4.2g
starch	57.5g
Fibre – NSP	6.95g
Sodium	423.75mg

VARIATION

Tip a 400g/14oz can of unsweetened chestnut purée into a bowl and beat it until softened. Stir the purée into the lentil mixture, with extra stock if required. Proceed as in the main recipe.

Mushroom and Sunflower Seed Flan

Mushrooms, baby corn and spinach make a delectable filling for a flan, especially when sunflower seeds are included.

INGREDIENTS

Serves 6

175g/6oz/1½ cups wholemeal flour
75g/3oz/6 tbsp low-fat spread
45ml/3 tbsp olive oil
175g/6oz baby corn, each cut into
  2–3 pieces
30ml/2 tbsp sunflower seeds
225g/8oz/2 cups mushrooms
75g/3oz fresh spinach leaves,
  chopped
juice of 1 lemon
sea salt and ground black pepper
tomato salad, to serve

1 Preheat the oven to 180°C/350°F/ Gas 4. Sift the flour into a bowl, then add the bran from the sieve. Rub in the low-fat spread until the mixture resembles breadcrumbs. Add enough water to make a firm dough.

2 Roll out the dough on a lightly floured surface and line a 23cm/9in flan dish. Prick the base, line the flan case with foil and add a layer of baking beans. Bake blind for 15 minutes, then remove the foil and beans. Return the pastry case to the oven and bake for a further 10 minutes, or until the pastry is crisp and golden brown.

NUTRITION NOTES

Per portion:	
Energy	250kcals/1045kJ
Fat, total	16g
saturated fat	2.8g
polyunsaturated fat	3.85g
monounsaturated fat	8.25g
Carbohydrate	20.6g
sugar, total	1.45g
starch	19.1g
Fibre – NSP	4.05g
Sodium	434.5mg

3 Meanwhile, heat the oil in a heavy-based pan. Fry the corn with the sunflower seeds for 5–8 minutes until lightly browned all over.

COOK'S TIP

If the mushrooms are small, leave them whole or cut them in half or quarters.

4 Add the button mushrooms, lower the heat slightly and cook the mixture for 2–3 minutes, then stir in the chopped spinach. Cover the pan and cook for 2–3 minutes.

5 Sharpen the filling with a little lemon juice. Stir in salt and pepper to taste. Spoon into the flan case. Serve warm or cold with a tomato salad.

Wholemeal Pasta with Caraway Cabbage

Crunchy cabbage and Brussels sprouts are the perfect partners for pasta in this healthy dish.

INGREDIENTS

Serves 6
90ml/6 tbsp olive or sunflower oil
3 onions, roughly chopped
350g/12oz round white cabbage, roughly chopped
350g/12oz Brussels sprouts, trimmed and halved
10ml/2 tsp caraway seeds
15ml/1 tbsp chopped fresh dill
400ml/14fl oz/1²/₃ cups vegetable stock
200g/7oz/1³/₄ cups fresh or dried wholewheat pasta spirals
sea salt and ground black pepper
dill sprigs, to garnish

1 Heat the oil in a large saucepan and fry the onions over a low heat for 10 minutes until softened.

2 Add the cabbage and Brussels sprouts and cook for 2–3 minutes, then stir in the caraway seeds and dill. Pour in the stock and season with salt and pepper to taste. Cover and simmer for 5–10 minutes until the cabbage and sprouts are crisp-tender.

—— COOK'S TIP ——

If tiny baby Brussels sprouts are available they can be used whole for this dish.

3 Meanwhile, cook the pasta in a pan of lightly salted boiling water, following the package instructions, until just tender.

4 Drain the pasta, tip it into a bowl and add the cabbage mixture. Toss lightly, adjust the seasoning and serve.

—— NUTRITION NOTES ——

Per portion:	
Energy	227kcals/953kJ
Fat, total	9.6g
saturated fat	1.4g
polyunsaturated fat	1.5g
monounsaturated fat	5.75g
Carbohydrate	30g
sugar, total	7.65g
starch	21.6g
Fibre – NSP	6.9g
Sodium	53.5mg

Cauliflower and Broccoli with Tomato Sauce

A low-fat alternative to that old favourite, cauliflower cheese. The addition of broccoli to the cauliflower gives extra colour.

INGREDIENTS

Serves 6
1 onion, finely chopped
400g/14oz can chopped tomatoes
45ml/3 tbsp tomato purée
45ml/3 tbsp wholemeal flour
300ml/½ pint/1¼ cups skimmed milk
300ml/½ pint/1¼ cups water
1kg/2¼lb/6 cups mixed cauliflower and broccoli florets
sea salt and ground black pepper

1 Mix the onion, tomatoes and tomato purée in a small saucepan. Bring to the boil, lower the heat and simmer for 15–20 minutes.

2 Mix the flour to a paste with a little of the milk. Stir the paste into the tomato mixture, then gradually add the remaining milk and the water. Stir constantly until the mixture boils and thickens. Season to taste with salt and pepper. Keep the sauce hot.

3 Steam the cauliflower (or mixture of cauliflower and broccoli) over boiling water for 5–7 minutes or until the florets are just tender. Tip into a dish, pour over the tomato sauce and serve with extra pepper sprinkled over the top, if liked.

—— NUTRITION NOTES ——

Per portion:	
Energy	116kcals/491kJ
Fat, total	1.85g
saturated fat	0.4g
polyunsaturated fat	0.9g
monounsaturated fat	0.2g
Carbohydrate	16.1g
sugar, total	10.3g
starch	5.4g
Fibre – NSP	4.5g
Sodium	86.8mg

Red Pepper Risotto

The character of this delicious risotto depends on the type of rice you use. With arborio rice, the risotto should be moist and creamy. If you use brown rice, reduce the amount of liquid for a drier dish with a nutty flavour.

INGREDIENTS

Serves 6

3 large red peppers
30ml/2 tbsp olive oil
3 large garlic cloves, thinly sliced
1½ x 400g/14oz cans chopped tomatoes
2 bay leaves
1.2–1.5 litres/2–2½ pints/5–6¼ cups
  vegetable stock
450g/1lb/2½ cups arborio rice (Italian
  risotto rice) or brown rice
6 fresh basil leaves, snipped
sea salt and ground black pepper

1 Preheat the grill. Put the peppers in a grill pan and grill until the skins are blackened and blistered all over. Put them in a bowl, cover with several layers of damp kitchen paper and leave for 10 minutes. Peel off the skins, then slice the peppers, discarding the core and seeds.

2 Heat 30ml/2 tbsp of the oil in a wide, shallow pan. Add the garlic and tomatoes and cook over a gentle heat for 5 minutes, then add the pepper slices and bay leaves. Stir well and cook for 15 minutes more.

3 Pour the stock into a saucepan and heat it to simmering point. Stir the rice into the vegetable mixture and cook for 2 minutes, then add two or three ladlefuls of the hot stock. Cook, stirring occasionally, until the stock has been absorbed.

4 Continue to add stock in this way, making sure each addition has been absorbed before pouring in the next. When the rice is tender, season with salt and pepper to taste. Remove the pan from the heat, cover and leave to stand for 10 minutes before stirring in the basil and serving.

——— NUTRITION NOTES ———	
Per portion:	
Energy	387kcals/1635kJ
Fat, total	10.75g
saturated fat	1.73g
polyunsaturated fat	1.3g
monounsaturated fat	6.3g
Carbohydrate	69.2g
sugar, total	7.85g
starch	60.85g
Fibre – NSP	3.2g
Sodium	645mg

Stir-fried Vegetables with Cashew Nuts

Stir-frying is the perfect way of making a delicious, colourful – and very speedy meal.

INGREDIENTS

Serves 4

900g/2lb mixed vegetables (see Cook's Tip)
30–60ml/2–4 tbsp sunflower or olive oil
2 garlic cloves, crushed
15ml/1 tbsp grated fresh root ginger
50g/2oz/½ cup cashew nuts or 60ml/4 tbsp sunflower seeds, pumpkin seeds or sesame seeds
soy sauce
sea salt and ground black pepper

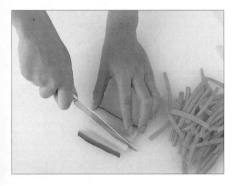

1 Prepare the vegetables according to type. Carrots and cucumber should be cut into very fine matchsticks.

2 Heat a frying pan, then trickle the oil around the rim so that it runs down to coat the surface. When it is hot, add the garlic and ginger and cook for 2–3 minutes, stirring. Add the harder vegetables and toss over the heat for 5 minutes until they start to soften.

3 Add the softer vegetables and stir-fry all of them over a high heat for about 3–4 minutes.

COOK'S TIP

Use a pack of stir-fry vegetables or make up your own mixture. Choose from carrots, mangetouts, baby sweetcorn, pak choy, cucumber, beansprouts, mushrooms, peppers and spring onions. Drained canned bamboo shoots and water chestnuts are delicious additions.

4 Stir in the cashew nuts or seeds. Season with soy sauce, salt and pepper to taste. Serve at once.

NUTRITION NOTES

Per portion:

Energy	288kcals/796kJ
Fat, total	21.3g
saturated fat	2.4g
polyunsaturated fat	8.3g
monounsaturated fat	9.3g
Carbohydrate	15.76g
sugar, total	9g
starch	5.2g
Fibre – NSP	5g
Sodium	170mg

DESSERTS

Desserts are always thought to be a no-go area for diabetics, but modern advice and the judicious use of fruits, mean that diabetics can now eat a wonderful range of desserts. Try, for example, a fruit flan with a tasty yogurt topping, a crumbly oat layer with strawberry filling or a delectable orange cheesecake. The recipes here are sweetened with fruits rather than sugar alternatives, which means that diabetics can absorb the sugar more easily. Nonetheless, it is important to remember that most desserts should only be eaten as occasional treats.

Baked Fruit Flan

Crisp pastry, juicy baked fruit and a delectable creamy yogurt and almond topping make this flan a family favourite.

INGREDIENTS

Serves 6
115g/4oz/1 cup wholemeal flour
50g/2oz/½ cup gram flour
50g/2oz/4 tbsp low-fat spread
about 45ml/3 tbsp cold water

For the filling and topping
15ml/1 tbsp liquid pear and
  apple concentrate
1 Bramley cooking apple
2 large oranges
3 kiwi fruit
300ml/½ pint/1¼ cups creamy Greek-
  style yogurt
15ml/1 tbsp browned flaked almonds

1 Preheat the oven to 180°C/350°F/ Gas 4. Mix the wholemeal and gram flours in a large mixing bowl and rub in the low fat spread with fingertips until the mixture resembles coarse breadcrumbs. Add just enough of the cold water to make a soft dough.

--- COOK'S TIP ---

To brown the almonds, spread them out in a grill pan and place them under a medium heat. Cook them until they are golden brown, shaking the pan frequently to make sure they brown on all sides. The process only takes a few minutes at most, so watch them closely in case they char.

2 Roll out the pastry on a lightly floured surface and use it to line a 20cm/8in round flan dish.

3 Prick the base of the pastry case with a fork, line it with foil and add a layer of baking beans. Bake blind for 15 minutes, then remove the foil and beans. Bake for 10 minutes more, until crisp. Remove the pastry case from the oven, but leave the oven on.

4 Carefully spread the pear and apple concentrate on the bottom of the pastry case. Peel and slice the apple, oranges and kiwi fruit.

5 Arrange the fruit in the pastry case, cover with foil and then bake for 20 minutes more. Leave to cool slightly.

6 Spoon the yogurt over the fruit in an even layer. Sprinkle the flaked almonds over the top. Serve the flan warm or at room temperature.

--- NUTRITION NOTES ---

Per portion:
Energy	254kcals/1070kJ
Fat, total	10.5g
saturated fat	3.8g
polyunsaturated fat	1.9g
monounsaturated fat	3.8g
Carbohydrate	31.9g
sugar, total	12.4g
starch	19.3g
Fibre – NSP	5g
Sodium	98mg

Hot Fruit Compote

The sugar content of this dessert is quite high, so serve it in small quantities along with a generous dollop of natural yogurt.

INGREDIENTS

Serves 8

450g/1lb/2½ cups mixed dried fruit, such as apricots, apples, prunes, large raisins, sultanas, figs and pears
475ml/16fl oz/2 cups water
thinly pared rind of 1 small lemon or 30ml/2 tbsp lemon juice
1 cinnamon stick
low-fat natural yogurt, to serve

1 Unless the fruit is of the ready-to-eat variety, soak overnight in the water, then drain, reserving the liquid.

2 Make up the liquid to 475ml/16fl oz/2 cups with water. Add the lemon rind or juice and the cinnamon.

3 Bring to the boil, lower the heat and add the drained fruit. Simmer for 15 minutes until the fruit is tender. Drain the fruit and transfer to a bowl. Return the syrup to the pan and simmer for 20 minutes until reduced slightly and thickened. Pour it over the fruit. Serve warm or cold, with yogurt.

--- NUTRITION NOTES ---

Per portion:	
Energy	118kcals/506kJ
Fat, total	0.35g
saturated fat	0g
polyunsaturated fat	0.05g
monounsaturated fat	0g
Carbohydrate	28.9g
sugar, total	28.9g
starch	0g
Fibre – NSP	4.6g
Sodium	15.1mg

Italian Fruit Salad and Ice Cream

If you visit Italy in the summer you will find little pavement fruit shops selling small dishes of macerated soft fruits, which are delectable on their own, but also make a wonderful ice cream.

INGREDIENTS

Serves 6

900g/2lb/8 cups mixed soft fruits, such as strawberries, raspberries, loganberries, redcurrants, blueberries, peaches, apricots, plums and melons
juice of 3–4 oranges
juice of 1 lemon
15ml/1 tbsp liquid pear and apple concentrate
60ml/4 tbsp whipping cream
30ml/2 tbsp orange-flavoured liqueur (optional)
mint sprigs, to decorate

1 Prepare the fruit according to type. Cut it into reasonably small pieces, but not so small that the mixture becomes a mush.

2 Put the fruit pieces in a serving bowl and pour over enough orange juice to cover. Add the lemon juice, stir gently, cover and chill for 2 hours.

3 Set half the macerated fruit aside to serve as it is. Purée the remainder in a blender or food processor.

--- COOK'S TIP ---

The macerated fruit makes a delicious drink. Purée then press through a strainer.

--- NUTRITION NOTES ---

Per portion:	
Energy	105kcals/332kJ
Fat, total	4.1g
saturated fat	2.5g
polyunsaturated fat	0.15g
monounsaturated fat	1.15g
Carbohydrate	13.5g
sugar, total	13.5g
starch	0g
Fibre – NSP	2.95g
Sodium	12.85mg

4 Gently warm the pear and apple concentrate and stir it into the fruit purée. Whip the cream and fold it in, then add the liqueur, if using.

5 Churn the mixture in an ice-cream maker. Alternatively, place it in a suitable container for freezing. Freeze until ice crystals form around the edge, then beat the mixture until smooth. Repeat the process once or twice, then freeze until firm. Soften slightly before serving in scoops decorated with mint accompanied by the macerated fruit.

Cranberry Rice Pudding

INGREDIENTS

Serves 4

300ml/½ pint/1¼ cups rice milk
1 vanilla pod
50g/2oz short-grain rice
40g/1½ oz/¼ cup cranberries

NUTRITION NOTES	
Per portion:	
Energy	71kcals/297kJ
Fat, total	1.6g
saturated fat	0.3g
polyunsaturated fat	0.8g
monounsaturated fat	0.4g
Carbohydrate	12g
sugar, total	1g
starch	11g
Fibre – NSP	0.4g
Sodium	25mg

1 Preheat the oven to 150°C/300°F/ Gas 2. Pour the rice milk into a small saucepan and add the vanilla pod. Bring the milk to just below boiling point, then remove the saucepan from the heat and leave the milk and vanilla to infuse for 10 minutes.

2 Put the rice and cranberries in a baking dish. Remove the vanilla pod from the milk, pour the milk into the dish and stir gently to mix lightly. Bake for 2½–3 hours, stirring from time to time. Serve the pudding warm or leave until cold.

Banana and Pineapple Ice Cream

INGREDIENTS

Serves 4

1 banana
150g/5oz fresh pineapple
150ml/¼ pint/⅔ cup low-fat
   natural yogurt
150ml/¼ pint/⅔ cup whipping cream,
   lightly whipped
sprig of mint, to garnish

NUTRITION NOTES	
Per portion:	
Energy	200kcals/832kJ
Fat, total	15.2g
saturated fat	9.5g
polyunsaturated fat	0.5g
monounsaturated fat	4.5g
Carbohydrate	13.5g
sugar, total	13g
starch	0.6g
Fibre – NSP	0.7g
Sodium	47mg

1 Purée the banana and pineapple in a blender or food processor. Tip the purée into a large bowl and stir in the natural yogurt. Fold in the cream.

VARIATION
Substitute the same quantity of drained canned pineapple in fruit juice for the fresh pineapple, or use fresh mango, instead.

2 Churn the mixture in an ice-cream maker. Alternatively, place it in a suitable container for freezering. Freeze until ice crystals form around the edges. Process or beat the mixture until it is smooth, then return it to the freezer.

3 Repeat the process once or twice, then freeze until firm. Remove from the freezer to soften slightly before serving, garnished with mint.

Apple and Banana Crumble

An old favourite, this crumble is naturally sweet with a crisp topping contrasting beautifully with the soft fruit. Bananas are delicious in a crumble, served with low-fat yogurt.

INGREDIENTS

Serves 6

2 large cooking apples
2 large bananas
60ml/4 tbsp water
50g/2oz/¼ cup low-fat spread
30–45ml/2–3 tbsp pear and
  apple spread
25g/1oz/¼ cup wholemeal flour
115g/4oz/1 cup porridge oats
30ml/2 tbsp sunflower seeds
low-fat yogurt, to serve (optional)

1 Preheat the oven to 180°C/350°F/ Gas 4. Cut the apples in quarters, remove the cores, then chop them into small pieces, leaving the skin on. Peel and slice the bananas. Mix the apples, bananas and water in a saucepan and cook until soft and pulpy.

2 Melt the low-fat spread with the pear and apple spread in a separate pan. Stir in the flour, oats and sunflower seeds and mix well.

3 Transfer the apple and banana mixture to an 18cm/7in baking dish and spread the oat crumble over the top. Bake for about 20 minutes or until the topping is golden brown. Serve warm or at room temperature, alone or with low-fat yogurt.

NUTRITION NOTES	
Per portion:	
Energy	181kcals/806kJ
Fat, total	7.36g
saturated fat	1.5g
polyunsaturated fat	2.9g
monounsaturated fat	2.5g
Carbohydrate	28.5g
sugar, total	12g
starch	16.3g
Fibre – NSP	3.2g
Sodium	58mg

Chocolate and Orange Mousse

There's no hint of deprivation in this divine dessert! It makes a great occasional treat, but eat with a high fibre main course.

INGREDIENTS

Serves 8

175g/6oz good-quality dark chocolate, broken into squares
grated rind and juice of 1½ large oranges, plus extra pared rind for decoration
5ml/1 tsp powdered gelatine
4 size 2 eggs, separated
90ml/6 tbsp unsweetened soya cream
60ml/4 tbsp brandy
chopped pistachio nuts, to decorate

1 Melt the chocolate in a heatproof bowl over a pan of hot water. Put 30ml/2 tbsp of the orange juice in a heatproof bowl and sprinkle the gelatine on top. When the gelatine is spongy, stand the bowl over a pan of hot water and stir until it has dissolved.

--- NUTRITION NOTES ---

Per portion:	
Energy	230kcals/966kJ
Fat, total	12.4g
saturated fat	4.6g
polyunsaturated fat	0.6g
monounsaturated fat	3.4g
Carbohydrate	17.3g
sugar, total	17g
Starch	0.2g
Fibre – NSP	0.55g
Sodium	113mg

2 Let the chocolate cool slightly, then beat in the orange rind, egg yolks, soya cream and brandy, followed by the gelatine mixture and the remaining orange juice. Set aside.

3 Whisk the egg whites in a grease-free bowl until they form soft peaks, then gently fold them into the chocolate and orange mixture.

4 Spoon or pour the mixture into six sundae dishes or glasses, or into a single glass bowl. Cover and chill until the mousse sets. Decorate with the chopped pistachio nuts and extra pared orange rind before serving.

Steamed Orange and Lemon Pudding

This delicious old-fashioned pudding tastes so good that you won't begrudge the time spent steaming it.

INGREDIENTS

Serves 8

115g/4oz/²⁄₃ cup raisins
60ml/4 tbsp brandy
115g/4oz/²⁄₃ cup dried, stoned dates
115g/4oz/½ cup low-fat spread
2 oranges
2 lemons
225g/8oz/2 cups self-raising
   wholemeal flour
5ml/1 tsp baking powder
3 size 2 eggs
1 pear, about 115g/4oz, peeled
   and puréed
250ml/8fl oz/1 cup low-fat
   fromage frais

1 Soak the raisins in the brandy in a small bowl. Meantime, put the dates in a separate bowl, add enough boiling water to cover them and leave to soak for 10 minutes. Drain the dates, chop them finely and place in a mixing bowl. Add the low-fat spread. Grate the rind from the oranges and lemons and add it to the bowl. Beat well.

2 Sift the flour with the baking powder. Gradually beat the eggs and pear purée into the creamed mixture, adding a little of the flour if the mixture shows signs of curdling.

3 Fold in the rest of the flour mixture, then the raisins with any remaining brandy. Spoon the mixture into a greased 900ml/1½ pint pudding basin. It should two-thirds fill it.

4 Cover the pudding basin with a pleated double layer of greaseproof paper tied firmly in place with string.

5 Stand the pudding basin on an inverted saucer in a large saucepan. Pour in enough boiling water to come halfway up the sides of the basin. Cover the saucepan tightly.

6 Steam the pudding in gently simmering water for 1½–2 hours, topping up the water from time to time. Squeeze the juice from one of the oranges and both the lemons. Put the fromage frais in a bowl and gradually beat in the citrus juice. Turn the pudding out on to a warmed serving plate and serve with the citrus sauce.

NUTRITION NOTES	
Per portion:	
Energy	303kcals/1280kJ
Fat, total	8.8g
saturated fat	2.4g
polyunsaturated fat	1.85g
monounsaturated fat	3.65g
Carbohydrate	45g
sugar, total	23.9g
starch	21.15g
Fibre – NSP	2.4g
Sodium	323mg

Peach and Raspberry Yogurt Fool

Low-fat, low-sugar natural or fruit yogurt makes an excellent basis for this delicious, quick and healthy dessert.

INGREDIENTS

Serves 4
2 peaches
225g/8oz raspberries
4 x 150ml/5fl oz pots low-fat natural or low-fat, low-sugar fruit yogurt
20ml/4 tsp porridge oats
20ml/4 tsp flaked almonds

1 Cut the peaches in half, remove the stones and then slice the flesh into thin wedges.

2 Mix the peaches and raspberries with the yogurt in a bowl, then spoon into four sundae glasses and chill.

3 Spread out the porridge oats and almonds in a grill pan. Grill them until lightly toasted, shaking the pan frequently. Cool, then sprinkle the oat mixture over the dessert and serve.

— VARIATION —

This works well with strawberries, apricots, kiwi fruit, pears, bananas or pineapple chunks. Match with a fruit yogurt of the same flavour, or a complementary variety.

— NUTRITION NOTES —

Per portion:

Energy	165kcals/699kJ
Fat, total	4.65g
saturated fat	1.1g
polyunsaturated fat	0.95g
monounsaturated fat	2.25g
Carbohydrate	21.65g
sugar, total	18.3g
starch	3.4g
Fibre – NSP	2.95g
Sodium	128mg

Strawberry Oat Crunch

This looks good and tastes delicious. The strawberries form a tasty filling between the layers of oat crumble.

INGREDIENTS

Serves 6
150g/5oz/1¼ cups porridge oats
50g/2oz/½ cup wholemeal flour
75g/3oz/6 tbsp low-fat spread
30ml/2 tbsp liquid pear and apple concentrate
500g/1¼lb strawberries
10ml/2 tsp arrowroot
low-fat yogurt or unsweetened soya cream, to serve

— VARIATION —

Use dried apricots (chop half and cook the rest to a purée with a little apple juice). Add chopped almonds to the crumble.

1 Preheat the oven to 180°C/350°F/Gas 4. Mix the oats and flour in a bowl. Melt the low-fat spread with the concentrate in a pan; stir into the bowl.

2 Purée half the strawberries in a food processor; chop the rest. Mix the arrowroot with a little of the purée in a small pan, then add the rest of the purée. Heat gently until thickened, then stir in the chopped strawberries.

3 Spread half the crumble mixture over the bottom of an 18cm/7in round shallow baking dish to form a layer at least 1cm/½in thick. Top with the strawberry mixture, then the remaining crumble, patting it down gently. Bake the crunch for 30 minutes. Serve warm or cold, alone or with low-fat yogurt or soya cream.

— NUTRITION NOTES —

Per portion:

Energy	208kcals/874kJ
Fat, total	7.65g
saturated fat	1.85g
polyunsaturated fat	2.25g
monounsaturated fat	3.05g
Carbohydrate	31.35g
sugar, total	8.4g
starch	22.95g
Fibre – NSP	3.45g
Sodium	89.35

Plum, Apple and Banana Scone Pie

This is one of those simple, satisfying puddings that everyone enjoys. It is delicious hot or cold and can be served on its own or with low-fat natural yogurt.

INGREDIENTS

Serves 4
450g/1lb plums
1 sharp cooking apple, about 115g/4oz
1 large banana
150ml/ ¼ pint/ ⅔ cup water
115g/4oz/1 cup wholemeal flour, or half wholemeal and half plain flour
10ml/2 tsp baking powder
25g/1oz/3 tbsp raisins
about 60ml/4 tbsp soured milk or low-fat natural yogurt
low-fat natural yogurt, to serve

1 Preheat the oven to 180°C/350°F/ Gas 4. Cut the plums in half and ease out the stones. Peel, core and chop the apple, then slice the banana.

2 Mix the fruit in a saucepan. Pour in the water. Bring to simmering point and cook gently for 15 minutes or until the fruit is soft.

3 Spoon the fruit mixture into a pie dish. Level the surface.

4 Mix the flour, baking powder and raisins in a bowl. Add the chosen liquid and mix to a very soft dough.

5 Transfer the scone dough to a lightly floured surface and divide it into 6–8 portions, then pat them into flattish scones.

6 Cover the plum and apple mixture with the scones. Bake the pie for 40 minutes until the scone topping is cooked through. Serve the pie hot with natural yogurt, or leave it until cold.

NUTRITION NOTES	
Per portion:	
Energy	195kcals/831kJ
Fat, total	1g
saturated fat	0.2g
polyunsaturated fat	0.35g
monounsaturated fat	0.1g
Carbohydrate	43.6g
sugar, total	24.2g
starch	19.4g
Fibre – NSP	5.2g
Sodium	315.2mg

Baked Orange Cheesecake

Making this delicious baked cheesecake couldn't be simpler. There's no crumb crust, and the orange-cheese filling is matched with a tangy sauce.

INGREDIENTS

Serves 8

4 oranges
250ml/8fl oz/1 cup low-fat
  fromage frais
50g/2oz/²/₃ cup ground almonds
50g/2oz/¹/₃ cup potato flour
10ml/2 tsp almond essence
2.5ml/¹/₂ tsp grated nutmeg
3 eggs, separated
115g/4oz/²/₃ cup sultanas
5ml/1 tsp arrowroot

1 Preheat the oven to 180°C/350°F/ Gas 4. Grate the rind from one orange and squeeze it. Place the rind and juice in a food processor with the fromage frais, ground almonds, potato flour, almond essence and nutmeg. Whizz briefly, then transfer to a large mixing bowl.

2 Beat in the egg yolks and sultanas. Whisk the egg whites in a clean grease-free bowl, then fold them into the creamy mixture.

3 Line a 20cm/8in springform tin with greaseproof paper. Grease the paper lightly, then pour in the mixture and bake for 40 minutes or until the cheesecake has risen and set.

4 Set the cheesecake aside in the tin to cool, then unclip and remove the sides of the tin. Carefully slide the dessert on to a serving dish.

5 Put the arrowroot in a small bowl. Grate the rind from two of the remaining oranges, then squeeze all the remaining fruit. Add a little juice to the arrowroot to make a paste, then stir in the rest of the juice and the rind.

6 Pour the mixture into a saucepan and heat gently, stirring all the time until the mixture thickens slightly. Cool the sauce to room temperature, then serve it with the cheesecake.

NUTRITION NOTES	
Per portion:	
Energy	181kcals/765kJ
Fat, total	6.3g
saturated fat	1.15g
polyunsaturated fat	1.2g
monounsaturated fat	3.3g
Carbohydrate	24.6g
sugar, total	19.35g
starch	5.35g
Fibre – NSP	2.45g
Sodium	51mg

CAKES, BAKES
AND
CONFECTIONERY

*Fancy morning-coffee biscuits, tea-time
cakes and even after-dinner sweets are no
longer off the menu for diabetics, although
they still need to be included in a daily
allocation of carbohydrates. Flapjacks and
ginger biscuits make good snacks for
children as well as delicious coffee
accompaniments. Cakes flavoured with
apple and spices or chocolate and prunes
use fruits instead of sugar, as do the Fruit
and Nut Chocolates and Apple and Date
Balls. (Note: where recipes have a
nutritional breakdown for the whole cake,
divide them into whatever size portions
you want and calculate accordingly.)*

Passion Cake

Grated carrot keeps this cake beautifully moist, while adding to the sweetness of the fruit.

INGREDIENTS

Makes a 20cm/8in cake
115g/4oz/½ cup low-fat spread
3 eggs, beaten
115g/4oz/²⁄₃ cup dried, stoned dates,
    softened in boiling water if necessary
1 large carrot, about 150g/5oz,
    finely grated
1 large pear, about 175g/6oz, peeled,
    cored and puréed
175g/6oz/1½ cups wholemeal flour
10ml/2 tsp baking powder
10ml/2 tsp ground cinnamon
5ml/1 tsp grated nutmeg
2.5ml/½ tsp allspice
2.5ml/½ tsp salt
pared orange rind, to decorate

For the icing
30ml/2 tbsp pear and apple spread
200ml/7fl oz/scant 1 cup low-fat
    fromage frais
grated rind of 1 orange

1 Preheat the oven to 190°C/375°F/ Gas 5. Grease and flour a 20cm/8in springform cake tin.

COOK'S TIP

A food processor makes short work of preparing the carrot and pear. Use the finest grater attachment for the carrot, then switch to the stainless steel blade and purée the chopped (uncooked) pear flesh.

2 Cream the low-fat spread in a bowl. Gradually beat in the eggs and dates. Mix in the grated carrot and the pear purée. Alternatively, use a food processor to mix the ingredients, then transfer to a bowl.

3 Sift the flour with the baking powder, spices and salt, then fold the dry ingredients carefully into the creamed mixture.

4 Spoon the cake mixture into the prepared springform tin. Bake for 25 minutes or until the cake is firm to the touch. Remove the cake from the tin and transfer to a wire rack. Allow to cool completely before icing it.

5 To make the icing for the cake, heat the pear and apple spread in a small saucepan until it is just runny. Put the fromage frais in a bowl. Stir in the melted pear and apple spread and the grated orange rind.

6 Spread the icing evenly over the cake. Decorate the top with the pared orange rind and leave to set.

NUTRITION NOTES

Per cake:	
Energy	1520kcals/6384kJ
Fat, total	73g
saturated fat	20g
polyunsaturated fat	16g
monounsaturated fat	30g
Carbohydrate	176g
sugar, total	63g
starch	112g
Fibre – NSP	24.8g
Sodium	2264mg

Lemon and Walnut Cake

Don't stint on the lemon rind – it gives this cake a wonderful zesty tang that complements the flavour of the walnuts.

INGREDIENTS

Makes a 20cm/8in cake

1 large banana, about 150g/5oz
225g/8oz/1 cup low-fat spread
150g/5oz/scant 1 cup dried, stoned dates
5 size 2 eggs
300g/11oz/2³/₄ cups wholemeal flour, or half wholemeal and half plain white flour
75g/3oz/³/₄ cup walnut pieces
4 large lemons

1 Preheat the oven to 180°C/350°F/ Gas 4. Lightly grease a deep 20cm/8in loose-based or spring-form cake tin. Line the base of the tin with non-stick baking paper.

COOK'S TIPS

If the dried dates are very hard, soften them in boiling water for 10 minutes before draining and using.

Make sure that you buy plain dried dates and not the kind that are chopped and coated with sugar.

Look out for packets of walnut pieces in supermarkets, as they are usually much less expensive than either shelled walnuts or walnut halves.

2 Peel and chop the banana. Process with the low-fat spread and dates.

3 Add 1 egg and 15ml/1 tbsp of the flour to the creamed mixture. Process briefly to mix, then add the remaining eggs one at a time, each with a further 15ml/1 tbsp flour.

4 Scrape the mixture into a bowl and fold in the remaining flour, with the walnut pieces.

5 Grate the rind from three lemons and thinly pare the rind from the fourth (reserve for the decoration). Squeeze the juice from two lemons, then stir the grated lemon rind and juice into the mixture.

6 Spoon the mixture into the prepared tin. Bake for 50–60 minutes or until a fine skewer inserted in the centre of the cake comes out clean. Cool on a wire rack. Decorate with the pared lemon rind.

NUTRITION NOTES

Per cake:

Energy	2845kcals/11900kJ
Fat, total	163g
saturated fat	34g
polyunsaturated fat	62g
monounsaturated fat	55g
Carbohydrate	280g
sugar, total	90g
starch	190g
Fibre – NSP	34g
Sodium	1660mg

Apple and Cinnamon Cake

Moist and spicy, this is perfect for packed lunches or afternoon tea.

INGREDIENTS

Makes a 20cm/8in square cake

115g/4oz/½ cup low-fat spread, plus
  extra for greasing
200g/7oz/1¼ cups dried, stoned dates
1–2 tart eating apples or 1 cooking
  apple, about 225g/8oz
7.5ml/1½ tsp mixed spice
5ml/1 tsp ground cinnamon
2.5ml/½ tsp salt
75g/3oz/½ cup raisins
2 size 2 eggs, beaten
150g/5oz/1¼ cups wholemeal
  flour, sifted
115g/4oz/generous 1 cup gram flour,
  sifted with 10ml/2 tsp baking powder
175ml/6fl oz/¾ cup unsweetened
  coconut milk

1 Preheat the oven to 180°C/350°F/ Gas 4. Lightly grease a deep 20cm/8in square baking tin and line the base with non-stick baking paper. Combine the low-fat spread and the dates in a food processor. Peel, core and grate the apple or apples and add to the low-fat spread and date mixture with the mixed spice, cinnamon and salt. Process until thoroughly blended.

2 Scrape the apple and date mixture into a bowl and fold in the raisins and beaten eggs alternately with the flours, baking powder and coconut milk. Transfer to the prepared tin and smooth the surface level.

3 Bake for 30–40 minutes until dark golden and firm to the touch. A skewer inserted in the centre should come out clean. Cool the cake in the tin for 15 minutes before turning out on a wire rack to cool completely.

NUTRITION NOTES	
Per cake:	
Energy	2036kcals/8588kJ
Fat, total	72g
saturated fat	4.5g
polyunsaturated fat	18.5g
monounsaturated fat	28g
Carbohydrate	300g
sugar, total	150g
starch	147g
Fibre – NSP	34.4g
Sodium	2412mg

Banana Bread

The very ripe bananas that are often sold off cheaply in supermarkets are perfect for this tried and trusted favourite.

INGREDIENTS

Makes 1 loaf
115g/4oz/½ cup low-fat spread, plus extra for greasing
5ml/1 tsp bicarbonate of soda
225g/8oz/2 cups wholemeal flour
2 eggs, beaten
3 very ripe bananas
30–45ml/2–3 tbsp unsweetened coconut milk or soya milk

1 Preheat the oven to 180°C/350°F/ Gas 4. Grease and base line a 23 x 13cm/9 x 5in loaf tin. Cream the low-fat spread in a bowl until it is fluffy. Sift the bicarbonate of soda with the flour, then add to the creamed low-fat spread, alternately with the eggs.

NUTRITION NOTES

Per loaf:
Energy	1616kcals/5090kJ
Fat, total	66g
saturated fat	17.5g
polyunsaturated fat	15.2g
monounsaturated fat	26.5g
Carbohydrate	215g
sugar, total	70g
starch	145g
Fibre – NSP	23.5g
Sodium	2320mg

2 Peel the bananas and slice them into a bowl. Mash them well, then stir them into the cake mixture. Mix in the coconut milk or soya milk.

VARIATION

Sunflower seeds make a good addition to banana cake. Add about 50g/2oz/½ cup to the mixture just before baking.

3 Spoon the mixture into the loaf tin and level the surface with a spoon. Bake for about 1¼ hours or until a fine skewer inserted in the centre comes out clean. Cool on a wire rack.

Rich Fruit Cake

This makes a good Christmas or birthday cake, but its relatively high fat and natural sugar content means that it should be an occasional treat for diabetics.

INGREDIENTS

Makes a 20cm/8in cake

1 large orange, quartered and seeded, but not peeled
1 large lemon, quartered and seeded, but not peeled
1 large cooking apple, cored and quartered, but not peeled
90g/3½ oz/generous ½ cup stoned dates
75g/3oz/6 tbsp low-fat spread
75g/3oz/6 tbsp hazelnut butter
90g/3½ oz/generous ½ cup raisins
90g/3½ oz/generous ½ cup currants
90g/3½ oz/generous ½ cup sultanas
90g/3½ oz/generous ½ cup ready-to-eat stoned prunes, chopped
50g/2oz/⅔ cup broken cashew nuts
5ml/1 tsp ground cinnamon
5ml/1 tsp grated nutmeg
2.5ml/½ tsp mace
2.5ml/½ tsp ground cloves
115g/4oz/1 cup wholemeal flour
7.5ml/1½ tsp baking powder
115g/4oz/1 cup porridge oats, processed until smooth
3 large eggs, beaten
45–60ml/3–4 tbsp unsweetened coconut or rice milk, if needed

— NUTRITION NOTES —	
Per cake:	
Energy	3087kcals/12990kJ
Fat, total	125g
saturated fat	30g
polyunsaturated fat	27g
monounsaturated fat	56g
Carbohydrate	440g
sugar, total	285g
starch	160g
Fibre – NSP	38g
Sodium	2200mg

1 Preheat the oven to 150°F/300°C/Gas 2. Grease and line a deep 20cm/8in round cake tin.

2 Combine the orange, lemon and apple in a food processor. Add the dates, vegetable fat and nut butter and process to a rough purée.

3 Scrape the mixture into a bowl and stir in the raisins, currants, sultanas, prunes, nuts and spices.

4 Stir in the flour, baking powder and porridge oats, alternately with the beaten eggs.

5 If the mixture seems very dry, stir in the coconut milk or rice milk.

6 Spoon the cake mixture into the prepared tin and bake for 1 hour or until a fine skewer inserted in the centre comes out clean. Leave to cool on a wire rack.

Fruit Malt Bread

INGREDIENTS

Makes 1 loaf

250g/9oz/2¼ cups self-raising
   wholemeal flour
pinch of salt
2.5ml/½ tsp bicarbonate of soda
175g/6oz/1 cup dried fruit
15ml/1 tbsp malt extract
250ml/8fl oz/1 cup skimmed milk
low-fat spread, to serve (optional)

COOK'S TIP

Use any combination of dried fruit you
like for this bread, choose from sultanas,
raisins and currants, or include chopped
dried pears, apricots, peaches or mangoes.

1 Preheat the oven to 160°C/325°F/
Gas 3. Grease a 23 x 13cm/9 x 5in
loaf tin. Line the base with non-stick
baking paper. Sift the flour, salt and
bicarbonate of soda into a bowl. Stir in
the dried fruit.

2 Heat the malt extract and milk in a
small saucepan, stirring until the
malt extract has dissolved. Tip it into
the dry ingredients and mix well.

3 Spoon the mixture into the
prepared tin. Bake for 45 minutes
or until a fine skewer inserted in the
loaf comes out clean. Cool on a wire
rack. Serve in slices, alone or with a
low-fat spread.

NUTRITION NOTES

Per loaf:	
Energy	1330kcals/5670kJ
Fat, total	6.5g
saturated fat	1g
polyunsaturated fat	2.5g
monounsaturated fat	7.5g
Carbohydrate	295g
sugar, total	138g
starch	155g
Fibre – NSP	26g
Sodium	1015mg

Chocolate and Prune Cake

Thanks to the gram flour, this delicious cake is high in soluble fibre although it is also quite high in sugar, so enjoy it as an occasional treat.

INGREDIENTS

Makes a 20cm/8in cake
300g/11oz dark chocolate
150g/5oz/²⁄₃ cup low-fat spread
200g/7oz/generous 1 cup ready-to-eat
   stoned prunes, quartered
3 eggs, beaten
150g/5oz/1¼ cups gram flour, sifted
   with 10ml/2 tsp baking powder
120ml/4fl oz/½ cup coconut milk,
   rice milk or soya milk

1 Preheat the oven to 180°C/350°F/ Gas 4. Grease and base-line a deep 20cm/8in round cake tin. Melt the chocolate in a heatproof bowl over a saucepan of hot water.

2 Mix the low-fat spread and prunes in a food processor. Process until light and fluffy, then scrape into a bowl.

3 Gradually fold in the melted chocolate and eggs, alternately with the flour mixture. Beat in the coconut milk, rice milk or soya milk.

——— COOK'S TIP ———

Use dark chocolate with a high proportion of cocoa solids (70%) for this cake.

4 Spoon the mixture into the cake tin, level the surface with a spoon, then bake for 20–30 minutes or until the cake is firm to the touch. A fine skewer inserted in the cake should come out clean. Leave to cool on a wire rack before serving.

NUTRITION NOTES	
Per cake:	
Energy	3178kcals/13315kJ
Fat, total	174g
saturated fat	74g
polyunsaturated fat	24g
monounsaturated fat	63g
Carbohydrate	340g
sugar, total	260g
starch	72g
Fibre – NSP	35g
Sodium	2640mg

Chocolate Brownies

Dark and full of flavour, these brownies are irresistible. They make a good tea-time treat, or are perfect for accompanying a cup of coffee with friends.

INGREDIENTS

Makes 20

150g/5oz/²⁄₃ cup low-fat spread
150g/5oz/scant 1 cup stoned dates, softened in boiling water, then drained and finely chopped
150g/5oz/1¼ cups self-raising wholemeal flour
10ml/2 tsp baking powder
60ml/4 tbsp cocoa powder dissolved in 30ml/2 tbsp hot water
60ml/4 tbsp apple and pear spread
90ml/6 tbsp unsweetened coconut milk
50g/2oz/½ cup walnuts or pecan nuts, roughly broken

1 Preheat the oven to 160°C/325°F/ Gas 3 and grease a 28 x 18cm/ 11 x 7in shallow baking tin. Cream the low-fat spread with the dates. Sift the flour with the baking powder, then fold into the creamed mixture, alternately with the cocoa, apple and pear spread and coconut milk. Stir in the nuts.

2 Spoon the mixture into the prepared tin, smooth the surface and bake for about 45 minutes or until a fine skewer inserted in the centre comes out clean. Cool for a few minutes in the tin, then cut into bars or squares. Cool on a wire rack.

——— Nutrition Notes ———	
Per brownie:	
Energy	91kcals/382kJ
Fat, total	5.6g
saturated fat	1.4g
polyunsaturated fat	2g
monounsaturated fat	2g
Carbohydrate	8.3g
sugar, total	3.12g
starch	5.15g
Fibre – NSP	1.3g
Sodium	142mg

Spicy Sultana Muffins

Sunday breakfasts will never be the same again, once you have tried these delicious muffins! They are easy to prepare and take only a short time to bake.

INGREDIENTS

Makes 6

75g/3oz/6 tbsp low-fat spread
1 small egg
120ml/4fl oz/½ cup unsweetened coconut milk
150g/5oz/1¼ cups wholemeal flour
7.5ml/1½ tsp baking powder
5ml/1 tsp ground cinnamon
generous pinch of salt
115g/4oz/²⁄₃ cup sultanas

1 Preheat the oven to 190°C/375°F/ Gas 5. Grease six muffin or deep bun tins. Beat the low-fat spread, egg and coconut milk in a bowl.

2 Sift the flour, baking powder, cinnamon and salt over the beaten mixture. Fold in, then beat well. Fold in the sultanas. Divide among the tins.

3 Bake for 20 minutes or until the muffins have risen well and are firm to the touch. Cool slightly on a wire rack before serving.

——— Cook's Tip ———
These muffins taste equally good cold. They also freeze well, packed in freezer bags. To serve, leave them to thaw overnight, or defrost in a microwave, then warm them briefly in the oven.

——— Nutrition Notes ———	
Per muffin:	
Energy	123kcals/514kJ
Fat, total	6.3g
saturated fat	1.75g
polyunsaturated fat	1.35g
monounsaturated fat	2.65g
Carbohydrate	14.85g
sugar, total	14.35g
starch	0.5g
Fibre – NSP	0.4g
Sodium	278.5mg

Flapjacks

Perfect for picnics and packed lunches, these flapjacks are really crisp and crunchy.

INGREDIENTS

Makes 16
115g/4oz/ ½ cup low-fat spread
60ml/4 tbsp rice syrup
50g/2oz/ ½ cup wholemeal flour
225g/8oz/2 cups porridge oats
50g/2oz/ ²/₃ cup pine nuts

1 Preheat the oven to 180°C/350°F/ Gas 4. Line a 20cm/8in shallow baking tin with oiled foil. Melt the low-fat spread and rice syrup in a small saucepan over a low heat, then stir in the flour, porridge oats and pine nuts until well mixed.

2 Tip the mixture into the tin and pat it out evenly with your fingers. Press the mixture down lightly. Bake for 25–30 minutes until the flapjacks are lightly browned and crisp. Mark into squares while still warm. Cool slightly, then lift them out of the tin and cool on a wire rack.

——— COOK'S TIP ———

Do not let the syrup mixture boil or the flapjacks will be tacky rather than crisp.

——— NUTRITION NOTES ———

Per flapjack:
Energy	122kcals/513kJ
Fat, total	6.4g
saturated fat	1.2g
polyunsaturated fat	2.55g
monounsaturated fat	2.35g
Carbohydrate	14.3g
sugar, total	1.45g
starch	11.05g
Fibre – NSP	1.35g
Sodium	54.1mg

Ginger Biscuits

INGREDIENTS

Makes 8 gingerbread men or 10–12 biscuits
115g/4oz/1 cup plain flour, sifted
7.5ml/1½ tsp ground ginger
grated rind of 1 orange and 1 lemon
75ml/5 tbsp pear and apple spread
25g/1oz/2 tbsp low-fat spread
16 currants and 8 raisins, to
    decorate (optional)

——— NUTRITION NOTES ———

Per gingerbread man:
Energy	85kcals/360kJ
Fat, total	1.5g
saturated fat	0.4g
polyunsaturated fat	0.5g
monounsaturated fat	0.55g
Carbohydrate	17.25g
sugar, total	5.85g
starch	11.4g
Fibre – NSP	0.5g
Sodium	23.1mg

1 Preheat the oven to 180°C/350°F/ Gas 4. Mix the sifted flour, ginger and grated orange and lemon rind in a bowl. Melt the pear and apple spread and the low-fat spread in a small saucepan over a low heat.

2 As soon as the pear and apple spread and margarine mixture has melted, stir it into the dry ingredients. Mix to a firm dough in the bowl, then remove the dough, wrap it in clear film and chill for 2–3 hours.

3 Roll out the dough on a lightly floured surface to a thickness of about 5mm/¼in. Cut out gingerbread men, using a cutter or a template. Alternatively, stamp the dough into 10–12 rounds with a 7cm/2³/₄in cutter.

4 If making gingerbread men, give them currant eyes and raisin noses. Using the point of a knife, draw a mouth on each. Place the biscuits on a lightly floured baking sheet and bake for 8–10 minutes. Cool on a wire rack.

Fruit and Nut Chocolates

When beautifully boxed, these make perfect presents.

INGREDIENTS

Makes 20

50g/2oz ready-to-eat stoned prunes or dried apricots
50g/2oz/⅓ cup sultanas or raisins
25g/1oz/2 tbsp ready-to eat dried apples, figs or dates
25g/1oz/⅓ cup flaked almonds
25g/1oz/¼ cup hazelnuts or walnuts
30–60ml/2–4 tbsp lemon juice
50g/2oz good-quality dark chocolate

1 Chop the fruit and nuts in a food processor or blender until fairly small. Add 30ml/2 tbsp lemon juice and process again to mix. Scrape the mixture into a bowl, taste and add more lemon juice if needed.

2 Melt the chocolate in a heatproof bowl over simmering water. Roll the fruit mixture into small balls. Using tongs or two forks, roll the balls in the melted chocolate, then place them on oiled foil to cool and set. If the chocolate becomes too solid to work with, reheat it gently.

┌─────────── NUTRITION NOTES ───────────┐

Per chocolate:

Energy	42kcals/176kJ
Fat, total	2.3g
saturated fat	0.55g
polyunsaturated fat	0.8g
monounsaturated fat	0.8g
Carbohydrate	4.95g
sugar, total	4.85g
starch	0.05g
Fibre – NSP	0.5g
Sodium	1.9mg

Apple and Date Balls

INGREDIENTS

Makes 20

1kg/2¼lb cooking apples or pears
115g/4oz/⅔ cup dried, stoned dates
250ml/8fl oz/1 cup apple juice
5ml/1 tsp ground cinnamon
50g/2oz/½ cup finely chopped walnuts

┌─────────── NUTRITION NOTES ───────────┐

Per ball:

Energy	47kcals/198kJ
Fat, total	1.8g
saturated fat	0.15g
polyunsaturated fat	1.25g
monounsaturated fat	0.3g
Carbohydrate	7.6g
sugar, total	7.6g
starch	0g
Fibre – NSP	1g
Sodium	1.9mg

1 Halve the unpeeled fruit and place in a large heavy-based saucepan. Add the dates, apple juice and ground cinnamon. Cook over a very low heat, stirring occasionally, for 4–6 hours or until the mixture forms a dry paste. Scrape into a bowl and cool, then roll the mixture into bite-sized balls. Toast the nuts under the grill until golden.

2 Coat the balls in the nut mixture. Twist each ball in a sweet wrapper or cellophane; store in an airtight box.

┌─────────── VARIATION ───────────┐

Use half-and-half ground cinnamon and ginger instead of the 5ml/1 tsp cinnamon.

Wholemeal Cheese Scones

These are very good warm with a little sunflower margarine.

INGREDIENTS

Makes 15
450g/1lb/4 cups wholemeal flour
pinch of salt
10ml/2 tsp baking powder
115g/4oz Parmesan cheese,
  finely grated
50g/2oz/¼ cup sunflower margarine
150–300ml/¼–½ pint/²/₃–1¼ cups
  buttermilk (see Cook's Tip)

COOK'S TIP

If you cannot obtain buttermilk, sour skimmed milk by stirring in a generous squeeze of lemon juice. Let the mixture stand for about 10 minutes before using it.

1 Preheat the oven to 200°C/400°F/ Gas 6. Mix the flour, salt, baking powder and Parmesan cheese in a bowl and rub in the margarine with your fingertips until the mixture resembles breadcrumbs. Working quickly and lightly, stir in enough of the buttermilk to make a moist dough.

2 Pat out the dough on a lightly floured board to a thickness of about 4cm/1½ in.

3 Using a 7cm/2¾ in cutter, cut out 15 rounds. Place the rounds on a floured baking sheet and bake for about 10 minutes. The exact cooking time will depend on the depth of the scones. They should be well risen and lightly browned. Serve warm, cut in half, with a little sunflower margarine.

NUTRITION NOTES

Per scone:

Energy	160kcals/674kJ
Fat, total	5.95g
saturated fat	2.25g
polyunsaturated fat	1.55g
monounsaturated fat	1.7g
Carbohydrate	20.4g
sugar, total	1.65g
starch	18.8g
Fibre – NSP	2.7g
Sodium	196.6mg

Information File

FURTHER READING
Beat Sugar Craving
by Maryon Stewart – Vermilion
Diabetes – A New Guide
by Dr Rowan Hillson – Optima
Healing Foods
by Miriam Polunin – Dorling
Kindersley
Nutritional Medicine
by Dr Stephen Davies and Dr Alan
Stewart – Pan Books
The Diabetic Kids' Cookbook
by Jane Rossiter and Rosemary
Seddon – Optima
**The Inside Story on Food
& Health**
Subscription magazine with general
information on diet and nutrition and
a lot of original, tested, no added
sugar, low-fat, dairy-free recipes.
Available from:
Berrydales Publishers
5 Lawn Road
London NW3 2 XS
Tel: 020 7722 2866

HELPFUL ORGANIZATIONS
The main associations dealing with
diabetes. Helplines, magazines, research
material, etc.
**British Diabetic
Association**
10 Queen Anne's Street
London W1M OBD
Tel: 020 7323 1531
**Canadian Diabetic
Association**
15 Toronto Street
Suite 800
Toronto
Ontario M5C2E3
Tel: Freephone 1 (800) Banting
Diabetes Australia
National Office
5–7 Phipps Place
Deakin ACT 2615
Tel: Freephone 1 (800) 640 862
**South African Diabetes
Association**
PO Box 1715
Saxonwold 21342
Tel: 011 (788) 45 95

**Institute For Complementary
Medicine**
PO Box 194
London SE16 1QZ
Tel: 020 7237 5165
Register of qualified complementary
practitioners. Public referral service,
newsletter and research material.
Medic Alert Foundation
1 Bridge Wharf
156 Caledonian Road
London N1 9UU
Tel: 020 7833 3034
Emergency identification system for
people with diabetes, allergies or other
hidden medical problems.

SHORT GLOSSARY OF BASIC TERMS
Adrenalin – hormone produced by
the adrenal gland to combat physical or
nervous stress.
Arteriosclerosis – hardening up or
furring up of the arteries.
Blood glucose – glucose level in
the blood (also known as blood
sugar), usually elevated in the case
of diabetics.
Cystitis – inflammation of the bladder.
Diabetes Mellitus – condition where
the blood sugar level is above normal.
Diuretics – pills that increase
urination.
Glucose – simple sugar found in
carbohydrates providing one of the
main energy sources for the body.
Glycogen – the form in which
glucose is stored in the blood.
Glycosuria – sugar or glucose in the
urine.
Hyperglycaemia – too much sugar or
glucose in the blood.
Hypoglycaemia – too little sugar or
glucose in the blood.
Insulin – hormone produced in the
pancreas, which allows glucose to enter
the blood stream.
Insulin Dependent Diabetes – a
condition in which the pancreas stops
producing insulin. The only treatment
is injected insulin.
Insulin receptor – site on the surface
of a cell into which the insulin

"docks" in order to allow the glucose
to enter through the cell walls.
Juvenile onset diabetes – diabetes
starting in youth that is nearly always
insulin dependent.
Ketoacidosis – severe excess of
glucose in the blood due to a severe
insulin deficiency causing fat breakdown and ketone formation.
Ketones – products that result from fat
breakdown that, in turn, results from
severe insulin deficiency. They smell of
acetone and are a symptom of severe
hyperglycaemia.
Maturity onset diabetes – diabetes
that affects people over 30 and that is
not usually insulin dependent.
Neuropathy – an abnormality in the
functioning of the nerves. Autonomic
neuropathy is partial failure of the
nerves controlling automatic body
functions. Peripheral Neuropathy
means that the nerves in the arms and
legs are affected.
Non Insulin Dependent Diabetes –
a condition where the pancreas is still
producing insulin, but either it is not
producing enough or is not acting very
effectively. Can usually be treated with
diet and glucose-lowering drugs.
Pancreas – a gland that is found
behind the stomach but in front of the
backbone. The pancreas produces
insulin and other digestive hormones.
Polydipsia – drinking large amounts
of water.
Polyuria – passing excessive amounts
of water on a frequent basis.
Retinopathy – abnormality of retina
in the eye, often caused by diabetes.

Index